If Found…

This is a very precious book!
If you find it, please return to:

Name _____

Address _____

_____

_____

Tel _____

Email _____

Reward: _____

One Year
On Purpose Planner™

The Definitive Happy Journal!

Deirdre G. Maguire

Cover Design by: Olga Vynnychenko, Email: by.amber.design@gmail.com

Printed in the United Kingdom

First Printing, 2016

ISBN-13:978-1537545141
ISBN-10:1537545140

62 Middle Tollymore Rd.
Newcastle, BT33 0JJ
Northern Ireland
United Kingdom

www.deirdremaguire.com

Goireann Beirt Bóthar

Two Shorten the Road

Ancient Gaelic Proverb

What's it All About?

This exciting and powerful step-by-step personal restoration program is specifically designed to be easy to follow, yet fully comprehensive. Sidestepping the symptoms of our daily life challenges the PHP Self Mastery Program addresses and eliminates the root cause of what holds us back.

Each component, while designed as a stand-alone independent unit, is also tailored to form the fabric of an all-inclusive, sequential, fully comprehensive solution. It will both entertain and inspire you as you design and follow through on your ultimate life plan.

By learning how to generate balance and sustained fulfillment in your relationships, health, finances and career, you will be well equipped to confidently co-create the life you desire.

Entry Levels

- **Private One-to-One Sessions** *(Initially safe, ultimately empowered)*

  This first point of entry into the PHP Self Mastery Program is about finding and clearing whatever is holding you back from achieving what you want in your life.

- **30-Day Program** *(Moving forward)*

  Continue the momentum of your transformation with a powerful, engaging 30-day program from the comfort of your own home.

- **Personal Power and Transformation Weekend**
  (Commit. Connect. Create a better you)

  It's time to set yourself free. Learn how to take control of all areas of your life while connecting with like-minded people, in a safe, supportive environment. In this fun, dynamic, powerful live experience, Deirdre will show you how to confidently and easily move forward in your life towards success and sustainable happiness.

- **Cut and Paste Your Perfect Life** *(Going deeper)*

  Now that you have the foundation from Personal Power and Transformation Weekend, you have the opportunity to become confident and competent in using the tools to transform specific areas of your life. The 2-hour-a-week four-week course will give you a deeper understanding of the PHP tools, by providing practical guidance in addressing the four main areas of life: Health, Relationships, Finances, and Career.

- **3 Day Intensive** *(Giving you back to you!)*

  This private, bespoke experience is catered for the individual, and is specifically designed to meet your personal needs. Have you ever wished that you could have an expert with you, to guide and facilitate the changes you want to make – free from the distractions and interruptions of your daily life? This is your chance for the Ultimate Personalised One-to-One Intensive Coaching experience, as Deirdre's house guest, in luxury accommodation and exquisite surroundings!

For more details, visit: www.deirdremaguire.com

DEDICATION

I dedicate this journal to all my Habilitat* brothers and sisters,
past, present and future.

There are two things I've learned from Habilitat:

1. It's always about exchange.
2. The Universe has got my back – always!

For both these core beliefs that form the fabric of my fundamental truth,
I offer my humble gratitude.
Mahalo!

*Habilitat is a long-term residential drug and alcohol treatment centre in Hawaii;
and home to the FasterEFT bi-annual Transformation Marathon.*

www.habilitat.com

ACKNOWLEDGEMENT

Words cannot describe the gratitude I feel for my close friend, mentor,
and founder of FasterEFT, Robert G. Smith. Without Robert, this book, along
with all my work I'm so proud of, would still be lost somewhere in
the recesses of my imagination with no way to come into physical reality. Not
only has FasterEFT enabled me to free myself to live the life I love now;
but Robert's support, guidance and friendship has been priceless in compelling
me to become the person I am today. Robert, I am eternally
grateful for all that you are, all that you have done and all that you
continue to bring to this great adventure we call life.

Welcome Friend!

As Part of my PHP Self Mastery Program™ It is my delight to introduce you to my **One Year On Purpose Planner™** *The Definitive Happy Journal!*

Well it's yours now actually so let me say, Congratulations on taking the first step towards a better life!

The Power House of Peace Self Mastery Program™ represents the culmination of my personal journey work which, by giving me emotional power and control, has taken me from "fear to fabulous" and an inner peace that previously I couldn't even dream of.

This *On Purpose Planner™* is a core component.

Although the *PHP Self Mastery Program™* houses my key modality FasterEFT, based on what I had learned about how the mind and body works I knew it was not enough to make changes just once.

The best results would come when, as well as using my tapping practice to let go of what now longer served me, I would make a conscious decision to get into a state of gratitude on a daily basis. I would also spend time bringing my attention to my intention for what I wanted to attract into my world. (founded on my 7 life enhancing core beliefs see - *The PHP Pillars of Truth* on page 23).

That's what I did in my journal and the results have been profound. During that year I added other components, which are listed on page 15. This powerful combination was a recipe for dynamic transformation.

"Your Freedom is my Promise" is something I say with conviction. This *On Purpose Planner™* is part of that promise.

They say it's not too crowded along the extra mile but if you are ready to do your work, I can tell you now it will definitely be worth it.

And as I tell my many clients across the globe (and now I'm telling you) I do not have to be physically with you to love and support you.

I really can see the diamond that you are…

Good luck, Much love and Peace always ,

Deirdre xx

"Whatever you can do, or dream you can, begin it. Boldness has genius, power, and magic in it."

Johann Wolfgang Von Goethe

Contents

Why Clever People Use This On Purpose Planner

Using this planner is about more than just having something to keep you on track. It's about more than just feeling good. Apart from the physical actions you take and the goals you achieve by using this planner, giving yourself the gift of your OPP will have a powerful effect on your overall health and happiness.

The Power of the On Purpose Planner

Here's a snapshot of the science that makes using your On Purpose Planner a no-brainer (pardon the pun!)

Fight-Flight-Freeze

A negative emotion is a chemical signal that your body has gone into a state of emergency (known as fight-flight-freeze). This causes your limbic brain and major organs to produce stress chemicals like *adrenaline* and *cortisol*. These emergency chemicals cause certain protective responses in your body. Blood is pumped away from your organs to your extremities - for fighting or running away; any processes that are not necessary for fighting or escaping are reduced or shut down. This includes: digestion, healing, cellular regrowth, and the absorption of nutrients into the cells.

Neuroscientist, Dr. Joe Dispenza uses the analogy of a country going to war. All resources are focused on defence, and nothing is available for growth, education, art, and industry.

Your Brain

During this fight-or-flight state, **part of the brain shuts down.** The prefrontal cortex is where you do your cognitive thinking – it's the part of the brain responsible for problem-solving, communication, noticing opportunities, taking advantage of them, and processing information. For this reason, whenever you are in a negative emotional state, **you are literally unable to think effectively.**

In normal circumstances, the emergency ends, and balance is restored. But the sensory overload of modern-day stress-filled living results in an unrelenting state of fight-or-flight. It is the impact of these **highly toxic chemicals** that make consistent commitment to your OPP (**the antidote**) not an optional extra but *your top priority.*

The Science of Feeling Good

Every time you have a positive thought, the connection in the neocortex of your brain causes the limbic part of your brain to produce endorphins and other **"feel-good" chemicals.** As these chemicals course through your blood stream, they affect your body in a variety of ways, including: lowering your blood pressure; allowing your organs to receive the blood flow (and with it, the oxygen and nutrients) they need to function optimally; reinstating digestion and healing; allowing the prefrontal cortex to come **back online** – and **with it, full functioning cognitive thinking!**

The Role of Your On Purpose Planner

Apart from helping you on a practical level, to plan and achieve the life you want within the next year, the On Purpose Planner is designed to help you to keep your brain and body chemistry balanced and in a **prime state for best results.**

Using this planner every day will ensure that you are able to spend **more time in positive emotional states,** than you do in negative. And this will have a direct effect on your body and brain – and therefore on the choices and decisions you make, along with the actions you take.

See? I told you – no-brainer! That's why I know you've already made the decision to invest in you by using this book.

Remind yourself, as you go through this planner, that by **taking physiological control of your emotions,** you are planning and achieving **your dream life.**

Say "CHEESE"!

What I often say to clients at the beginning of their journey of
transformation / restoration is:
Take a selfie today - you won't recognise yourself in six months' time!
The truth is that the mind is reflected in the body; and as we clear out the limiting
beliefs we've been holding within, we begin to lighten up; look better;
feel better; and this is expressed in our outward appearance.
The inside transformed – is reflected on the outside!
So, before you go any further, take a selfie (tap if you need to!), print it out,
and place it in the space below.

DAY 1

DAY 365

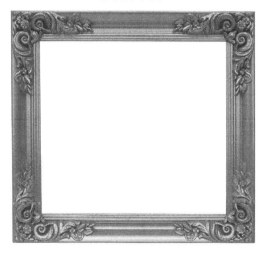

PHP Self Mastery Steps

1. I am aware …. that something needs to change.
2. I am coming to believe that change is possible.
3. I am ready to take a look.
4. I am making the decision to move forward.
5. I am ready for change.
6. I want change.
7. I embrace change.
8. I am ready to talk about change with others.
9. I am taking responsibility for my own happiness.
10. I know I am on the journey.
11. I remember to remember.
12. I know I make a difference.

"The Wound is the place where the light enters you."
~ Sufi poet Rumi

What You Believe to Be True, is True for You

Why I Created the Pillars of Truth

When I understood what was happening in a moment of crises, and I realised that it wasn't about what the other person was seemingly doing to me, but actually what I was believing about myself in that moment, I knew it was time to create a better set of beliefs. The **PHP Self Mastery Pillars of Truth** are the result.

Affirming these, every day, in addition to using FasterEFT, has served to replace old limiting beliefs with a set of empowering, life-enhancing principles. And if I can do it, you can do it too!

1. I am the Expression of Life.

2. You are the Expression of Life.

3. We are all One.

4. Life Source has got my back – always.

5. I am safe.

6. I belong.

7. I serve.

How to Get the Most from Your OPP

"We are what we repeatedly do. Excellence then is not an act, but a habit." ~ Aristotle 384-322 BC

The Validity of the Law of Repetition is nothing new. However, with the advent of groundbreaking equipment like the M.R.I. and C.T. scans we now have proof of its effects. Science can now confirm that while initiating new behaviour is an essential first step to a better quality of life, it is commitment to repetition that sustains it. Replicating new behavior serves 2 purposes. It creates a new neural pattern in the brain and causes the old neural one to 'drop off'. That's why it makes sense for you to write up your 3 Gratitude's and your Gratitude Intentions every day for a year.

Gratitude for what you already have. (Your health, your home, your food etc.)

Gratitude Intentions i.e. getting grateful for that which you are attracting into your life. (Your new partner, your successful business, your deeper inner peace).

It makes sense to add descriptive emotion when you are doing this. Emotions are the juice that transports the thought from the mind to make it real in the body aka a 'state'. Then these ideas, plans and dreams go from your page to your life. Remember ***EVERY THING STARTS WITH A THOUGHT.*** This is the fundamental first step.

For example:

Gratitude

I am so grateful for the beautiful blue skies, the gorgeous clouds and the fabulous mountains.

I am so grateful for my life, my friends, my health and all that's so amazing in my life.

Gratitude Intention

I am so grateful that I get to enjoy the excitement of travel. I am so delighted to be able to take care of myself in a kind and caring way.

I love my 3-day intensive Transformation Experience that helps so many people.

Journaling. Happy Stuff. Photos.

Journaling

This part of your OPP is intended to serve as a Personal Record of what's actually going on in your mind and later on to show you how far you've come.

This section is designed to help you pay attention to and articulate what is going on in your mind. Take a few minutes to give time to watching your thoughts, writing them and seeing what's going on when you slow your process down a little. This is a way of honouring yourself. You will look back and see how far you've come, how much you've grown. You choose if you want to make this a daily practice.

Happy Stuff. Photos.

This part of your OPP is intended to serve as a place to collect, create and remind you of positive emotional states.

Break things up a little by keeping some happy memorabilia here. Tickets from fun times out, photos etc. that remind you of good people in your life, fun times etc. I like handwritten envelopes from birthday cards (as well as the card!) I put them here. I also have a pretty napkin my mum gave me on an afternoon tea visit to her home. It typifies her and reminds me how much I love her when I see it.

So this sums up your daily visit to your OPP.

Perhaps the most important aspect of this work is to remember to **be nice to you.** Too often in my personal experience and also working with clients, I watched where people start off with great enthusiasm only to give up at the first hurdle. The secret to the success of this is to keep going. Get back up again. Begin again. If you miss a day, rather than beating yourself up, go to the current page and then go back another time when you are bursting with so much to be grateful for to the unfilled page. This is priceless wisdom. Use it.

The other exercises are designed to supplement and support you in creating and following through on your 12-month ultimate life plan.

Good luck,
Peace always,
Deirdre x

Your Personal Mission Statement

Who you are and how you can express yourself in the world is directed by your essence. This is your connection with and contribution to the world. Let this simple exercise help you get clear.

Answer these questions with a short statement for each:

1. What do you want most out of life?
E.g. to be happy and feel fulfilled

2. What do you want to see happen in the world?
E.g. peace and happiness

3. What makes YOU special?
E.g. my energy and enthusiasm

4. What are you capable of doing right now?
E.g. Writing, public speaking parenting

Now write your statement by combining from above as follows:

I will (Choose from your answers to question 4)

_____

_____

Using my (from your answers to question 3)

_____

_____

To accomplish (from your answers to question 2)

_____

_____

And in so doing achieve (from your answers to question 1)

_____

_____

How to Tap

Tapping is a 4-step process

1. **Aim**
2. **Tap**
3. **Breathe**
4. **Peace**

Aim. *Notice how you know.*

> Notice any sensations in the body.
> Notice any emotions you may have.
> Notice any pictures or sounds in your mind.

Tap. *Using 2 fingers tap 2 or 3 times on the meridian points.*

> Notice the sensations of your fingers tapping on your body.
> Take your attention away from the problem in your mind,
> to the physical sensations of your fingers as you say, "Let it go."

Breathe. *Grab your wrist.*

> Take your attention to your breath and breathe in and out.

Peace. *Take your attention to a happy place or memory.*

> While still holding your wrist say **"Peace."**

Repeat until emotional intensity is zero.

Check if the old memory is gone.

Flip to a positive. Replace old problem/memory with a positive.

* For more information on FasterEFT tapping, visit:
www.deirdremaguire.com or www.youtube.com/wisdomofireland

Goals
"I'm so happy now that..."

"Man cannot do right in one department of life whilst he is occupied doing wrong in any other department. Life is one indivisible whole." ~ Mahatma Ghandi

Learning

This exercise is designed to bring your awareness to every aspect of your life. This will help you to create and maintain balance. We are beginning to set your internal Sat Nav/GPS so you can create your life by design not default.

This is one of the most crucial components in order to get you to where you currently are not!

When working with a client I will say this: Imagine we are planning to go for a drive today. Full of excitement we jump into the car – and then we look at one another. "Where do you want go?" I say, to which the client replies "I don't know! " Well then we can't leave the driveway! But if I say Dublin or Belfast and the client makes the decision for Dublin – then it's easy! We know to turn left out of the drive, right at the top of the road, left at the junction then we head to Newry then Dundalk and its all good! We may even meet some sheep on the way (-it IS Ireland after all!) but we don't mind because *we know where we're going!* And it's the same for our internal life gps /sat nav. When we know where we are going and what we want our lives to look like then the drifting has stopped, the decision fatigue ends, the stress declines and we are setting ourselves up for success. There is just the beginning but it's a great start.

Action /Exercise

Instruction: *Read this out loud daily for 30 days. In front of a mirror is an additional option, which I highly recommend. It's what I do. Tap on any resistance.*

Assuming the feeling of the wish fulfilled is critical here i.e. pretend/ act as if you are already living the life you want. *Remember Everything – (and I mean **Everything**) starts with a thought.* The car, the telephone, the iPhone® all started as a thought in someone's head. This is your beginning. **Go for it.**

I'm so happy now that my calling excites, delights and fulfills me on a daily basis. What I love most about my calling is that I am on purpose. The way my calling supports and contributes to the other areas of my life is excellent, fulfilling and so very exciting.

I'm so happy now that I enjoy great connection in my life. As I reach out to others I make a conscious decision to create and connect with friends. I speak to people in line. I say hello to someone who seems to be alone. I smile at people in the street. I offer to help people. I make this a priority in my life. I have a great sense of my belonging in the world. I love and support as much as I would like to be loved and supported and this makes me feel good inside.

I'm so happy now that I make my contribution to the world. Serving others through playing my part in sustaining goodness on the planet makes me feel alive. This reminds me of the vital role we all play and that I really do belong. Allowing others the honour of contribution by kindly receiving from them allows the balance of flow and reminds me that **We are all One.**

I'm so happy now that my finances are so very healthy. Money supplies all my needs on a daily basis. Because I know **the universe has got my back always,** I give and receive easily.

I'm so happy now that fun turns up in some form or other every day. Whether I am with friends, family or colleagues or on my own, my capacity to generate joy from within myself and to have a laugh increases daily.

I'm so happy now that I enjoy optimal health. I honour my body by learning and understanding how it works. I appreciate good food and I eat healthily. I respect and honour my body by exercising and resting on a daily basis.

I'm so happy now that personal growth plays its part in my life. I find what works for me and feed my habit by learning and growing every day.

I'm so happy now that I engage in spiritual practice within my day-to-day living. I give time to quiet reflection and gentle inner awareness and so I give myself permission to enjoy balance and peace in each present moment.

Affirmations
(Positive)

"Affirmations are statements going beyond the reality of the present into the creation of the future through the words you use in the now." ~Louise L. Hay

The affirmations exercise, saying positive phrases either out loud or in the mind, is very familiar in the world of personal development.

What most people do not realize is that everything we say is an affirmation! For example *'I can't lose weight', 'I'm stupid', 'I'm always messing it up'* or *'There I go again!'*

A favourite of mine was to say to *"you stupid b**ch!"* either in my head or quite often out loud! When I learned that everything is an affirmation I changed this to *"ah ya wee pet!"* Do not underestimate the power of this practice.

My initial post cancer experience was peppered with anxiety as I had to face yet another tragic cancer story in my day-to-day living. At this time I created the affirmation *"My body knows EXACTLY how to heal"* which I would use to counteract any stress in my body.

Others I like are:

> *'I am healthy wealthy and wise.'*
> *'I love easily.'*
> *'I am complete.'*
> *'I am guided.'*
> *'I am taken care of.'*
> *'My resources are abundant.'*

Create what works for you and write them in your OPP. You can also record them with inspirational music and play them as you fall asleep.

Because we know that affirmations are what we believe or want to believe I invite you to make good use of my most powerful ones *The PHP Self Mastery Pillars* of Truth (page 23).

'AHA' Moments
Illumination Outbursts!

Definition:
"A moment of sudden realization, inspiration, insight, recognition, or comprehension"

These are a couple of my AHA moments:

'The day I realized I threw out birthday cards and kept bank statements.'

'The Pearl out of the Pain. The day I realized the pain of going to work for another day was pushing me to make better decisions for myself.'

This page serves 2 purposes: one to record your growth and secondly to reflect on your progress!

_____

_____

_____

_____

_____

_____

_____

_____

_____

_____

_____

_____

_____

Midget Gems
The forever kind!

Midget Gems was the name given to a popular jelly sweet when I was growing up, so I used the title to record short sweet sayings that have impacted my life. Such as:

'This too shall pass'.
'You are no longer alone'.
'History is only as good as the story teller.'

As you begin to do your personal work and continue to open up your mind, your own sweet gems will come into your awareness. Mine have stayed with me till this day and have served me very well. I trust you will enjoy yours!

Poetry Emotion

"Poetry is the Art of uniting pleasure with truth."
~Samuel Johnson 1709-1784

The title of this section is a play on the title of the song *"Poetry in Motion"*, a U.K. number-one hit single in 1961.

And just as song can stir deep emotions within us so too can a great poem elicit powerful passion and profound sentiment. This section is for you to find and record yours.

Here is one of my favourites for you as an example:

The Stranger Who was Yourself

The time will come
When, with elation
You will greet yourself arriving
at your own door, in your own mirror
And each will smile at the other's welcome,

And say, sit here. Eat.
You will love again the stranger who was your self.
Give wine. Give bread. Give back your heart
to itself, to the stranger who has loved you

All your life, whom you ignored
for another, who knows you by heart.
Take down the love letters from the bookshelf,

The photographs, the desperate notes,
Peel your own image from the mirror.
Sit. Feast on your life.

Derek Walcott

My Support Network

"Acting on the need for help is finally taking hold of the gift of ownership and allowing radical transformation to begin"
~ Deirdre Maguire, Mind Wellness Expert

This is where you make a list of people you will go to, turn to, when you need to connect or ask for help.

In my work I have typically found people who are very good at helping others yet find it difficult to ask for support themselves.

On this list I have put personal friends and then local groups I belong to. You can put your church if you belong to one and mentors and people you admire.

If you haven't already done so I encourage you to reach out and consciously join a local group to either participate or volunteer. We are tribal and we need to connect.

_____

_____

_____

_____

_____

_____

_____

_____

_____

_____

_____

_____

_____

_____

Inspired Melodies

"Without music, life would be a mistake"
~ Friedrich Wilhelm Nietzsche (1844–1900), German philosopher

Inspirational music and songs have transformed the mood and mindset of generations forever. Using this powerful tool is very clever.

This page is for writing your go to list of songs that move you. The key is then to use this list as an easy reference and reminder when you need.

_____

_____

_____

_____

_____

_____

_____

_____

_____

_____

_____

_____

_____

_____

_____

_____

_____

Daily Journal - Day 1 / 365

Today is _____ / _____ / _____

My Gratitudes:

1. _____

2. _____

3. _____

My Gratitude Intentions - Setting my GPS / SAT NAV:

1. _____

2. _____

3. _____

Journaling. Happy Stuff. Photos. (Or extra Gratitude!)

What limits my life most are the bars of destructive thought, which cage me in. Released from these I am free to exhaust the endless possibilities of my joy!

Daily Journal - Day 2 / 364

Today is _____ / _____ / _____

My Gratitudes:

1. _____

2. _____

3. _____

My Gratitude Intentions - Setting my GPS / SAT NAV:

1. _____

2. _____

3. _____

Journaling. Happy Stuff. Photos. (Or extra Gratitude!)

Daily Journal - Day 3 / 363

Today is _____ / _____ / _____

My Gratitudes:

1. _____

2. _____

3. _____

My Gratitude Intentions - Setting my GPS / SAT NAV:

1. _____

2. _____

3. _____

Journaling. Happy Stuff. Photos. (Or extra Gratitude!)

Daily Journal - Day 4 / 362

Today is _____ / _____ / _____

My Gratitudes:

1. _____

2. _____

3. _____

My Gratitude Intentions - Setting my GPS / SAT NAV:

1. _____

2. _____

3. _____

Journaling. Happy Stuff. Photos. (Or extra Gratitude!)

Daily Journal - Day 5 / 361

Today is _____ / _____ / _____

My Gratitudes:

1. _____

2. _____

3. _____

My Gratitude Intentions - Setting my GPS / SAT NAV:

1. _____

2. _____

3. _____

Journaling. Happy Stuff. Photos. (Or extra Gratitude!)

Daily Journal - Day 6 / 360

Today is _____ / _____ / _____

My Gratitudes:

1. _____

2. _____

3. _____

My Gratitude Intentions - Setting my GPS / SAT NAV:

1. _____

2. _____

3. _____

Journaling. Happy Stuff. Photos. (Or extra Gratitude!)

My life is my own flick book. What I choose to think, and
so what I choose to do, day-by-day, is what I choose to become.

Daily Journal - Day 7 / 359

Today is _____ / _____ / _____

My Gratitudes:

1. _____

2. _____

3. _____

My Gratitude Intentions - Setting my GPS / SAT NAV:

1. _____

2. _____

3. _____

Journaling. Happy Stuff. Photos. (Or extra Gratitude!)

Daily Journal - Day 8 / 358

Today is _____ / _____ / _____

My Gratitudes:

1. _____

2. _____

3. _____

My Gratitude Intentions - Setting my GPS / SAT NAV:

1. _____

2. _____

3. _____

Journaling. Happy Stuff. Photos. (Or extra Gratitude!)

Daily Journal - Day 9 / 357

Today is _____ /_____ /_____

My Gratitudes:

1. _____

2. _____

3. _____

My Gratitude Intentions - Setting my GPS / SAT NAV:

1. _____

2. _____

3. _____

Journaling. Happy Stuff. Photos. (Or extra Gratitude!)

Daily Journal - Day 10 / 356

Today is _____ / _____ / _____

My Gratitudes:

1. _____

2. _____

3. _____

My Gratitude Intentions - Setting my GPS / SAT NAV:

1. _____

2. _____

3. _____

Journaling. Happy Stuff. Photos. (Or extra Gratitude!)

Daily Journal - Day 11 / 355

Today is _____ / _____ / _____

My Gratitudes:

1. _____

2. _____

3. _____

My Gratitude Intentions - Setting my GPS / SAT NAV:

1. _____

2. _____

3. _____

Journaling. Happy Stuff. Photos. (Or extra Gratitude!)

Daily Journal - Day 12 / 354

Today is _____ / _____ / _____

My Gratitudes:

1. _____

2. _____

3. _____

My Gratitude Intentions - Setting my GPS / SAT NAV:

1. _____

2. _____

3. _____

Journaling. Happy Stuff. Photos. (Or extra Gratitude!)

Daily Journal - Day 13 / 353

Today is _____ / _____ / _____

My Gratitudes:

1. _____

2. _____

3. _____

My Gratitude Intentions - Setting my GPS / SAT NAV:

1. _____

2. _____

3. _____

Journaling. Happy Stuff. Photos. (Or extra Gratitude!)

Make gratitude my quiet daily practice that comes with me to every situation.

Daily Journal - Day 14 / 352

Today is _____ / _____ / _____

My Gratitudes:

1. _____

2. _____

3. _____

My Gratitude Intentions - Setting my GPS / SAT NAV:

1. _____

2. _____

3. _____

Journaling. Happy Stuff. Photos. (Or extra Gratitude!)

Daily Journal - Day 15 / 351

Today is _____ / _____ / _____

My Gratitudes:

1. _____

2. _____

3. _____

My Gratitude Intentions - Setting my GPS / SAT NAV:

1. _____

2. _____

3. _____

Journaling. Happy Stuff. Photos. (Or extra Gratitude!)

Daily Journal - Day 16 / 350

Today is _____ / _____ / _____

My Gratitudes:

1. _____

2. _____

3. _____

My Gratitude Intentions - Setting my GPS / SAT NAV:

1. _____

2. _____

3. _____

Journaling. Happy Stuff. Photos. (Or extra Gratitude!)

Daily Journal - Day 17 / 349

Today is _____ / _____ / _____

My Gratitudes:

1. _____

2. _____

3. _____

My Gratitude Intentions - Setting my GPS / SAT NAV:

1. _____

2. _____

3. _____

Journaling. Happy Stuff. Photos. (Or extra Gratitude!)

Daily Journal - Day 18 / 348

Today is _____ / _____ / _____

My Gratitudes:

1. _____

2. _____

3. _____

My Gratitude Intentions - Setting my GPS / SAT NAV:

1. _____

2. _____

3. _____

Journaling. Happy Stuff. Photos. (Or extra Gratitude!)

Daily Journal - Day 19 / 347

Today is _____ / _____ / _____

My Gratitudes:

1. _____

2. _____

3. _____

My Gratitude Intentions - Setting my GPS / SAT NAV:

1. _____

2. _____

3. _____

Journaling. Happy Stuff. Photos. (Or extra Gratitude!)

Right now I am rallying. Though pain plays its impostor part, that which is alive in me responds, regroups, reforms - despite my insignificant fears.

Daily Journal - Day 20 / 346

Today is _____ / _____ / _____

My Gratitudes:

1. _____

2. _____

3. _____

My Gratitude Intentions - Setting my GPS / SAT NAV:

1. _____

2. _____

3. _____

Journaling. Happy Stuff. Photos. (Or extra Gratitude!)

Daily Journal - Day 21 / 345

Today is _____ /_____ /_____

My Gratitudes:

1. _____

2. _____

3. _____

My Gratitude Intentions - Setting my GPS / SAT NAV:

1. _____

2. _____

3. _____

Journaling. Happy Stuff. Photos. (Or extra Gratitude!)

Daily Journal - Day 22 / 344

Today is _____ /_____ /_____

My Gratitudes:

1. _____

2. _____

3. _____

My Gratitude Intentions - Setting my GPS / SAT NAV:

1. _____

2. _____

3. _____

Journaling. Happy Stuff. Photos. (Or extra Gratitude!)

Daily Journal - Day 23 / 343

Today is _____ / _____ / _____

My Gratitudes:

1. _____

2. _____

3. _____

My Gratitude Intentions - Setting my GPS / SAT NAV:

1. _____

2. _____

3. _____

Journaling. Happy Stuff. Photos. (Or extra Gratitude!)

Daily Journal - Day 24 / 342

Today is _____ / _____ / _____

My Gratitudes:

1. _____

2. _____

3. _____

My Gratitude Intentions - Setting my GPS / SAT NAV:

1. _____

2. _____

3. _____

Journaling. Happy Stuff. Photos. (Or extra Gratitude!)

Daily Journal - Day 25 / 341

Today is _____ / _____ / _____

My Gratitudes:

1. _____

2. _____

3. _____

My Gratitude Intentions - Setting my GPS / SAT NAV:

1. _____

2. _____

3. _____

Journaling. Happy Stuff. Photos. (Or extra Gratitude!)

When I finally dare to view the true nature of my death I let the serenity of surrender wash over the precious currency of my one and only life.

Daily Journal - Day 26 / 340

Today is _____ / _____ / _____

My Gratitudes:

1. _____

2. _____

3. _____

My Gratitude Intentions - Setting my GPS / SAT NAV:

1. _____

2. _____

3. _____

Journaling. Happy Stuff. Photos. (Or extra Gratitude!)

Daily Journal - Day 27 / 339

Today is _____ / _____ / _____

My Gratitudes:

1. _____

2. _____

3. _____

My Gratitude Intentions - Setting my GPS / SAT NAV:

1. _____

2. _____

3. _____

Journaling. Happy Stuff. Photos. (Or extra Gratitude!)

Daily Journal - Day 28 / 338

Today is _____ / _____ / _____

My Gratitudes:

1. _____

2. _____

3. _____

My Gratitude Intentions - Setting my GPS / SAT NAV:

1. _____

2. _____

3. _____

Journaling. Happy Stuff. Photos. (Or extra Gratitude!)

Daily Journal - Day 29 / 337

Today is _____ / _____ / _____

My Gratitudes:

1. _____

2. _____

3. _____

My Gratitude Intentions - Setting my GPS / SAT NAV:

1. _____

2. _____

3. _____

Journaling. Happy Stuff. Photos. (Or extra Gratitude!)

Daily Journal - Day 30 / 336

Today is _____ / _____ / _____

My Gratitudes:

1. _____

2. _____

3. _____

My Gratitude Intentions - Setting my GPS / SAT NAV:

1. _____

2. _____

3. _____

Journaling. Happy Stuff. Photos. (Or extra Gratitude!)

Daily Journal - Day 31 / 335

Today is _____ /_____ /_____

My Gratitudes:

1. _____

2. _____

3. _____

My Gratitude Intentions - Setting my GPS / SAT NAV:

1. _____

2. _____

3. _____

Journaling. Happy Stuff. Photos. (Or extra Gratitude!)

Daily Journal - Day 32 / 334

Today is _____ / _____ / _____

My Gratitudes:

1. _____

2. _____

3. _____

My Gratitude Intentions - Setting my GPS / SAT NAV:

1. _____

2. _____

3. _____

Journaling. Happy Stuff. Photos. (Or extra Gratitude!)

As I scan the time line of my soul's earth journey from above I choose to catch the countless gems of love sparkling with the glint of life's magic!

Daily Journal - Day 33 / 333

Today is _____ / _____ / _____

My Gratitudes:

1. _____

2. _____

3. _____

My Gratitude Intentions - Setting my GPS / SAT NAV:

1. _____

2. _____

3. _____

Journaling. Happy Stuff. Photos. (Or extra Gratitude!)

Daily Journal - Day 34 / 332

Today is _____ / _____ / _____

My Gratitudes:

1. _____

2. _____

3. _____

My Gratitude Intentions - Setting my GPS / SAT NAV:

1. _____

2. _____

3. _____

Journaling. Happy Stuff. Photos. (Or extra Gratitude!)

Daily Journal - Day 35 / 331

Today is _____ / _____ / _____

My Gratitudes:

1. _____

2. _____

3. _____

My Gratitude Intentions - Setting my GPS / SAT NAV:

1. _____

2. _____

3. _____

Journaling. Happy Stuff. Photos. (Or extra Gratitude!)

Daily Journal - Day 36 / 330

Today is _____ / _____ / _____

My Gratitudes:

1. _____

2. _____

3. _____

My Gratitude Intentions - Setting my GPS / SAT NAV:

1. _____

2. _____

3. _____

Journaling. Happy Stuff. Photos. (Or extra Gratitude!)

Daily Journal - Day 37 / 329

Today is _____ / _____ / _____

My Gratitudes:

1. _____

2. _____

3. _____

My Gratitude Intentions - Setting my GPS / SAT NAV:

1. _____

2. _____

3. _____

Journaling. Happy Stuff. Photos. (Or extra Gratitude!)

Daily Journal - Day 38 / 328

Today is _____ /_____ /_____

My Gratitudes:

1. _____

2. _____

3. _____

My Gratitude Intentions - Setting my GPS / SAT NAV:

1. _____

2. _____

3. _____

Journaling. Happy Stuff. Photos. (Or extra Gratitude!)

Daily Journal - Day 39 / 327

Today is _____ / _____ / _____

My Gratitudes:

1. _____

2. _____

3. _____

My Gratitude Intentions - Setting my GPS / SAT NAV:

1. _____

2. _____

3. _____

Journaling. Happy Stuff. Photos. (Or extra Gratitude!)

When I grease the cogs of my true knowing with the oil of my 5 star attitude my life moves effortlessly in the clear direction of my choice.

Daily Journal - Day 40 / 326

Today is _____ / _____ / _____

My Gratitudes:

1. _____

2. _____

3. _____

My Gratitude Intentions - Setting my GPS / SAT NAV:

1. _____

2. _____

3. _____

Journaling. Happy Stuff. Photos. (Or extra Gratitude!)

Daily Journal - Day 41 / 325

Today is _____ / _____ / _____

My Gratitudes:

1. _____

2. _____

3. _____

My Gratitude Intentions - Setting my GPS / SAT NAV:

1. _____

2. _____

3. _____

Journaling. Happy Stuff. Photos. (Or extra Gratitude!)

Daily Journal - Day 42 / 324

Today is _____ / _____ / _____

My Gratitudes:

1. _____

2. _____

3. _____

My Gratitude Intentions - Setting my GPS / SAT NAV:

1. _____

2. _____

3. _____

Journaling. Happy Stuff. Photos. (Or extra Gratitude!)

Daily Journal - Day 43 / 323

Today is _____ / _____ / _____

My Gratitudes:

1. _____

2. _____

3. _____

My Gratitude Intentions - Setting my GPS / SAT NAV:

1. _____

2. _____

3. _____

Journaling. Happy Stuff. Photos. (Or extra Gratitude!)

Daily Journal - Day 44 / 322

Today is _____ /_____ /_____

My Gratitudes:

1. _____

2. _____

3. _____

My Gratitude Intentions - Setting my GPS / SAT NAV:

1. _____

2. _____

3. _____

Journaling. Happy Stuff. Photos. (Or extra Gratitude!)

Daily Journal - Day 45 / 321

Today is _____ / _____ / _____

My Gratitudes:

1. _____

2. _____

3. _____

My Gratitude Intentions - Setting my GPS / SAT NAV:

1. _____

2. _____

3. _____

Journaling. Happy Stuff. Photos. (Or extra Gratitude!)

Peace comes beautifully to me when I allow myself to steal into the quiet recesses of my gentle soul and rest in the comfort of my Divine Connection.

Daily Journal - Day 46 / 320

Today is _____ / _____ / _____

My Gratitudes:

1. _____

2. _____

3. _____

My Gratitude Intentions - Setting my GPS / SAT NAV:

1. _____

2. _____

3. _____

Journaling. Happy Stuff. Photos. (Or extra Gratitude!)

Daily Journal - Day 47 / 319

Today is _____ / _____ / _____

My Gratitudes:

1. _____

2. _____

3. _____

My Gratitude Intentions - Setting my GPS / SAT NAV:

1. _____

2. _____

3. _____

Journaling. Happy Stuff. Photos. (Or extra Gratitude!)

Daily Journal - Day 48 / 318

Today is _____ / _____ / _____

My Gratitudes:

1. _____

2. _____

3. _____

My Gratitude Intentions - Setting my GPS / SAT NAV:

1. _____

2. _____

3. _____

Journaling. Happy Stuff. Photos. (Or extra Gratitude!)

Daily Journal - Day 49 / 317

Today is _____ /_____ /_____

My Gratitudes:

1. _____

2. _____

3. _____

My Gratitude Intentions - Setting my GPS / SAT NAV:

1. _____

2. _____

3. _____

Journaling. Happy Stuff. Photos. (Or extra Gratitude!)

Daily Journal - Day 50 / 316

Today is _____ / _____ / _____

My Gratitudes:

1. _____

2. _____

3. _____

My Gratitude Intentions - Setting my GPS / SAT NAV:

1. _____

2. _____

3. _____

Journaling. Happy Stuff. Photos. (Or extra Gratitude!)

Daily Journal - Day 51 / 315

Today is _____ /_____ /_____

My Gratitudes:

1. _____

2. _____

3. _____

My Gratitude Intentions - Setting my GPS / SAT NAV:

1. _____

2. _____

3. _____

Journaling. Happy Stuff. Photos. (Or extra Gratitude!)

Abundance is what fills my life when I decide to finally cut the ties of my limited past, detach from the confines of my old pain and fill up at the fountain of all sustaining joy!

Daily Journal - Day 52 / 314

Today is _____ / _____ / _____

My Gratitudes:

1. _____

2. _____

3. _____

My Gratitude Intentions - Setting my GPS / SAT NAV:

1. _____

2. _____

3. _____

Journaling. Happy Stuff. Photos. (Or extra Gratitude!)

Daily Journal - Day 53 / 313

Today is _____ / _____ / _____

My Gratitudes:

1. _____

2. _____

3. _____

My Gratitude Intentions - Setting my GPS / SAT NAV:

1. _____

2. _____

3. _____

Journaling. Happy Stuff. Photos. (Or extra Gratitude!)

Daily Journal - Day 54 / 312

Today is _____ / _____ / _____

My Gratitudes:

1. _____

2. _____

3. _____

My Gratitude Intentions - Setting my GPS / SAT NAV:

1. _____

2. _____

3. _____

Journaling. Happy Stuff. Photos. (Or extra Gratitude!)

Daily Journal - Day 55 / 311

Today is _____ / _____ / _____

My Gratitudes:

1. _____

2. _____

3. _____

My Gratitude Intentions - Setting my GPS / SAT NAV:

1. _____

2. _____

3. _____

Journaling. Happy Stuff. Photos. (Or extra Gratitude!)

Daily Journal - Day 56 / 310

Today is _____ / _____ / _____

My Gratitudes:

1. _____

2. _____

3. _____

My Gratitude Intentions - Setting my GPS / SAT NAV:

1. _____

2. _____

3. _____

Journaling. Happy Stuff. Photos. (Or extra Gratitude!)

Daily Journal - Day 57 / 309

Today is _____ / _____ / _____

My Gratitudes:

1. _____

2. _____

3. _____

My Gratitude Intentions - Setting my GPS / SAT NAV:

1. _____

2. _____

3. _____

Journaling. Happy Stuff. Photos. (Or extra Gratitude!)

The gap between my expectations and what is has the measure of my greatest pain. When I engage in total acceptance I lavish total joy upon myself!

Daily Journal - Day 58 / 308

Today is _____ / _____ / _____

My Gratitudes:

1. _____

2. _____

3. _____

My Gratitude Intentions - Setting my GPS / SAT NAV:

1. _____

2. _____

3. _____

Journaling. Happy Stuff. Photos. (Or extra Gratitude!)

Daily Journal - Day 59 / 307

Today is _____ / _____ / _____

My Gratitudes:

1. _____

2. _____

3. _____

My Gratitude Intentions - Setting my GPS / SAT NAV:

1. _____

2. _____

3. _____

Journaling. Happy Stuff. Photos. (Or extra Gratitude!)

Daily Journal - Day 60 / 306

Today is _____ / _____ / _____

My Gratitudes:

1. _____

2. _____

3. _____

My Gratitude Intentions - Setting my GPS / SAT NAV:

1. _____

2. _____

3. _____

Journaling. Happy Stuff. Photos. (Or extra Gratitude!)

Daily Journal - Day 61 / 305

Today is _____ / _____ / _____

My Gratitudes:

1. _____

2. _____

3. _____

My Gratitude Intentions - Setting my GPS / SAT NAV:

1. _____

2. _____

3. _____

Journaling. Happy Stuff. Photos. (Or extra Gratitude!)

Daily Journal - Day 62 / 304

Today is _____ / _____ / _____

My Gratitudes:

1. _____

2. _____

3. _____

My Gratitude Intentions - Setting my GPS / SAT NAV:

1. _____

2. _____

3. _____

Journaling. Happy Stuff. Photos. (Or extra Gratitude!)

Daily Journal - Day 63 / 303

Today is _____ / _____ / _____

My Gratitudes:

1. _____

2. _____

3. _____

My Gratitude Intentions - Setting my GPS / SAT NAV:

1. _____

2. _____

3. _____

Journaling. Happy Stuff. Photos. (Or extra Gratitude!)

*When I engage with my highest awareness and use the Power invested in me
I stand tall and mighty in the ranks of an invincible Universal strength
made all the more unique by its benign gentility.*

Daily Journal - Day 64 / 302

Today is _____ / _____ / _____

My Gratitudes:

1. _____

2. _____

3. _____

My Gratitude Intentions - Setting my GPS / SAT NAV:

1. _____

2. _____

3. _____

Journaling. Happy Stuff. Photos. (Or extra Gratitude!)

Daily Journal - Day 65 / 301

Today is _____ / _____ / _____

My Gratitudes:

1. _____

2. _____

3. _____

My Gratitude Intentions - Setting my GPS / SAT NAV:

1. _____

2. _____

3. _____

Journaling. Happy Stuff. Photos. (Or extra Gratitude!)

Daily Journal - Day 66 / 300

Today is _____ / _____ / _____

My Gratitudes:

1. _____

2. _____

3. _____

My Gratitude Intentions - Setting my GPS / SAT NAV:

1. _____

2. _____

3. _____

Journaling. Happy Stuff. Photos. (Or extra Gratitude!)

Daily Journal - Day 67 / 299

Today is _____ /_____ /_____

My Gratitudes:

1. _____

2. _____

3. _____

My Gratitude Intentions - Setting my GPS / SAT NAV:

1. _____

2. _____

3. _____

Journaling. Happy Stuff. Photos. (Or extra Gratitude!)

Daily Journal - Day 68 / 298

Today is _____ / _____ / _____

My Gratitudes:

1. _____

2. _____

3. _____

My Gratitude Intentions - Setting my GPS / SAT NAV:

1. _____

2. _____

3. _____

Journaling. Happy Stuff. Photos. (Or extra Gratitude!)

Daily Journal - Day 69 / 297

Today is _____ / _____ / _____

My Gratitudes:

1. _____

2. _____

3. _____

My Gratitude Intentions - Setting my GPS / SAT NAV:

1. _____

2. _____

3. _____

Journaling. Happy Stuff. Photos. (Or extra Gratitude!)

The walk of experience is the treadmill of my life bringing me to a level of inner fitness of Olympian standard.

Daily Journal - Day 70 / 296

Today is _____ / _____ / _____

My Gratitudes:

1. _____

2. _____

3. _____

My Gratitude Intentions - Setting my GPS / SAT NAV:

1. _____

2. _____

3. _____

Journaling. Happy Stuff. Photos. (Or extra Gratitude!)

Daily Journal - Day 71 / 295

Today is _____ /_____ /_____

My Gratitudes:

1. _____

2. _____

3. _____

My Gratitude Intentions - Setting my GPS / SAT NAV:

1. _____

2. _____

3. _____

Journaling. Happy Stuff. Photos. (Or extra Gratitude!)

Daily Journal - Day 72 / 294

Today is _____ / _____ / _____

My Gratitudes:

1. _____

2. _____

3. _____

My Gratitude Intentions - Setting my GPS / SAT NAV:

1. _____

2. _____

3. _____

Journaling. Happy Stuff. Photos. (Or extra Gratitude!)

Daily Journal - Day 73 / 293

Today is _____ / _____ / _____

My Gratitudes:

1. _____

2. _____

3. _____

My Gratitude Intentions - Setting my GPS / SAT NAV:

1. _____

2. _____

3. _____

Journaling. Happy Stuff. Photos. (Or extra Gratitude!)

Daily Journal - Day 74 / 292

Today is _____ / _____ / _____

My Gratitudes:

1. _____

2. _____

3. _____

My Gratitude Intentions - Setting my GPS / SAT NAV:

1. _____

2. _____

3. _____

Journaling. Happy Stuff. Photos. (Or extra Gratitude!)

Daily Journal - Day 75 / 291

Today is _____ / _____ / _____

My Gratitudes:

1. _____

2. _____

3. _____

My Gratitude Intentions - Setting my GPS / SAT NAV:

1. _____

2. _____

3. _____

Journaling. Happy Stuff. Photos. (Or extra Gratitude!)

Practice is my most powerful act of personal responsibility.

Daily Journal - Day 76 / 290

Today is _____ / _____ / _____

My Gratitudes:

1. _____

2. _____

3. _____

My Gratitude Intentions - Setting my GPS / SAT NAV:

1. _____

2. _____

3. _____

Journaling. Happy Stuff. Photos. (Or extra Gratitude!)

Daily Journal - Day 77 / 289

Today is _____ / _____ / _____

My Gratitudes:

1. _____

2. _____

3. _____

My Gratitude Intentions - Setting my GPS / SAT NAV:

1. _____

2. _____

3. _____

Journaling. Happy Stuff. Photos. (Or extra Gratitude!)

Daily Journal - Day 78 / 288

Today is _____ / _____ / _____

My Gratitudes:

1. _____

2. _____

3. _____

My Gratitude Intentions - Setting my GPS / SAT NAV:

1. _____

2. _____

3. _____

Journaling. Happy Stuff. Photos. (Or extra Gratitude!)

Daily Journal - Day 79 / 287

Today is _____ / _____ / _____

My Gratitudes:

1. _____

2. _____

3. _____

My Gratitude Intentions - Setting my GPS / SAT NAV:

1. _____

2. _____

3. _____

Journaling. Happy Stuff. Photos. (Or extra Gratitude!)

Daily Journal - Day 80 / 286

Today is _____ / _____ / _____

My Gratitudes:

1. _____

2. _____

3. _____

My Gratitude Intentions - Setting my GPS / SAT NAV:

1. _____

2. _____

3. _____

Journaling. Happy Stuff. Photos. (Or extra Gratitude!)

Daily Journal - Day 81 / 285

Today is _____ / _____ / _____

My Gratitudes:

1. _____

2. _____

3. _____

My Gratitude Intentions - Setting my GPS / SAT NAV:

1. _____

2. _____

3. _____

Journaling. Happy Stuff. Photos. (Or extra Gratitude!)

Awareness, like the first tentative step of a child, is the fundamental foothold on the journey to my Joy.

Daily Journal - Day 82 / 284

Today is _____ / _____ / _____

My Gratitudes:

1. _____

2. _____

3. _____

My Gratitude Intentions - Setting my GPS / SAT NAV:

1. _____

2. _____

3. _____

Journaling. Happy Stuff. Photos. (Or extra Gratitude!)

Daily Journal - Day 83 / 283

Today is _____ / _____ / _____

My Gratitudes:

1. _____

2. _____

3. _____

My Gratitude Intentions - Setting my GPS / SAT NAV:

1. _____

2. _____

3. _____

Journaling. Happy Stuff. Photos. (Or extra Gratitude!)

Daily Journal - Day 84 / 282

Today is _____ /_____ /_____

My Gratitudes:

1. _____

2. _____

3. _____

My Gratitude Intentions - Setting my GPS / SAT NAV:

1. _____

2. _____

3. _____

Journaling. Happy Stuff. Photos. (Or extra Gratitude!)

Daily Journal - Day 85 / 281

Today is _____ / _____ / _____

My Gratitudes:

1. _____

2. _____

3. _____

My Gratitude Intentions - Setting my GPS / SAT NAV:

1. _____

2. _____

3. _____

Journaling. Happy Stuff. Photos. (Or extra Gratitude!)

Daily Journal - Day 86 / 280

Today is _____ / _____ / _____

My Gratitudes:

1. _____

2. _____

3. _____

My Gratitude Intentions - Setting my GPS / SAT NAV:

1. _____

2. _____

3. _____

Journaling. Happy Stuff. Photos. (Or extra Gratitude!)

Daily Journal - Day 87 / 279

Today is _____ /_____ /_____

My Gratitudes:

1. _____

2. _____

3. _____

My Gratitude Intentions - Setting my GPS / SAT NAV:

1. _____

2. _____

3. _____

Journaling. Happy Stuff. Photos. (Or extra Gratitude!)

To serve is not a giving up, rather it is a giving to,
where I am always the recipient.

Daily Journal - Day 88 / 278

Today is _____ / _____ / _____

My Gratitudes:

1. _____

2. _____

3. _____

My Gratitude Intentions - Setting my GPS / SAT NAV:

1. _____

2. _____

3. _____

Journaling. Happy Stuff. Photos. (Or extra Gratitude!)

Daily Journal - Day 89 / 277

Today is _____ / _____ / _____

My Gratitudes:

1. _____

2. _____

3. _____

My Gratitude Intentions - Setting my GPS / SAT NAV:

1. _____

2. _____

3. _____

Journaling. Happy Stuff. Photos. (Or extra Gratitude!)

Daily Journal - Day 90 / 276

Today is _____ / _____ / _____

My Gratitudes:

1. _____

2. _____

3. _____

My Gratitude Intentions - Setting my GPS / SAT NAV:

1. _____

2. _____

3. _____

Journaling. Happy Stuff. Photos. (Or extra Gratitude!)

Daily Journal - Day 91 / 275

Today is _____ /_____ /_____

My Gratitudes:

1. _____

2. _____

3. _____

My Gratitude Intentions - Setting my GPS / SAT NAV:

1. _____

2. _____

3. _____

Journaling. Happy Stuff. Photos. (Or extra Gratitude!)

Daily Journal - Day 92 / 274

Today is _____ / _____ / _____

My Gratitudes:

1. _____

2. _____

3. _____

My Gratitude Intentions - Setting my GPS / SAT NAV:

1. _____

2. _____

3. _____

Journaling. Happy Stuff. Photos. (Or extra Gratitude!)

Daily Journal - Day 93 / 273

Today is _____ / _____ / _____

My Gratitudes:

1. _____

2. _____

3. _____

My Gratitude Intentions - Setting my GPS / SAT NAV:

1. _____

2. _____

3. _____

Journaling. Happy Stuff. Photos. (Or extra Gratitude!)

Daily Journal - Day 94 / 272

Today is _____ / _____ / _____

My Gratitudes:

1. _____

2. _____

3. _____

My Gratitude Intentions - Setting my GPS / SAT NAV:

1. _____

2. _____

3. _____

Journaling. Happy Stuff. Photos. (Or extra Gratitude!)

I know that success tomorrow depends on how I choose to live today.

Daily Journal - Day 95 / 271

Today is _____ / _____ / _____

My Gratitudes:

1. _____

2. _____

3. _____

My Gratitude Intentions - Setting my GPS / SAT NAV:

1. _____

2. _____

3. _____

Journaling. Happy Stuff. Photos. (Or extra Gratitude!)

Daily Journal - Day 96 / 270

Today is _____ / _____ / _____

My Gratitudes:

1. _____

2. _____

3. _____

My Gratitude Intentions - Setting my GPS / SAT NAV:

1. _____

2. _____

3. _____

Journaling. Happy Stuff. Photos. (Or extra Gratitude!)

Daily Journal - Day 97 / 269

Today is _____ / _____ / _____

My Gratitudes:

1. _____

2. _____

3. _____

My Gratitude Intentions - Setting my GPS / SAT NAV:

1. _____

2. _____

3. _____

Journaling. Happy Stuff. Photos. (Or extra Gratitude!)

Daily Journal - Day 98 / 268

Today is _____ / _____ / _____

My Gratitudes:

1. _____

2. _____

3. _____

My Gratitude Intentions - Setting my GPS / SAT NAV:

1. _____

2. _____

3. _____

Journaling. Happy Stuff. Photos. (Or extra Gratitude!)

Daily Journal - Day 99 / 267

Today is _____ / _____ / _____

My Gratitudes:

1. _____

2. _____

3. _____

My Gratitude Intentions - Setting my GPS / SAT NAV:

1. _____

2. _____

3. _____

Journaling. Happy Stuff. Photos. (Or extra Gratitude!)

When I allow myself to go inside and touch My Source I connect up to the magical in me. And As I feed my habit I am free.

Daily Journal - Day 100 / 266

Today is _____ / _____ / _____

My Gratitudes:

1. _____

2. _____

3. _____

My Gratitude Intentions - Setting my GPS / SAT NAV:

1. _____

2. _____

3. _____

Journaling. Happy Stuff. Photos. (Or extra Gratitude!)

Daily Journal - Day 101 / 265

Today is _____ /_____ /_____

My Gratitudes:

1. _____

2. _____

3. _____

My Gratitude Intentions - Setting my GPS / SAT NAV:

1. _____

2. _____

3. _____

Journaling. Happy Stuff. Photos. (Or extra Gratitude!)

Daily Journal - Day 102 / 264

Today is _____ / _____ / _____

My Gratitudes:

1. _____

2. _____

3. _____

My Gratitude Intentions - Setting my GPS / SAT NAV:

1. _____

2. _____

3. _____

Journaling. Happy Stuff. Photos. (Or extra Gratitude!)

Daily Journal - Day 103 / 263

Today is _____ /_____ /_____

My Gratitudes:

1. _____

2. _____

3. _____

My Gratitude Intentions - Setting my GPS / SAT NAV:

1. _____

2. _____

3. _____

Journaling. Happy Stuff. Photos. (Or extra Gratitude!)

Daily Journal - Day 104 / 262

Today is _____ / _____ / _____

My Gratitudes:

1. _____

2. _____

3. _____

My Gratitude Intentions - Setting my GPS / SAT NAV:

1. _____

2. _____

3. _____

Journaling. Happy Stuff. Photos. (Or extra Gratitude!)

Daily Journal - Day 105 / 261

Today is _____ / _____ / _____

My Gratitudes:

1. _____

2. _____

3. _____

My Gratitude Intentions - Setting my GPS / SAT NAV:

1. _____

2. _____

3. _____

Journaling. Happy Stuff. Photos. (Or extra Gratitude!)

When I step into my world of true faith, I hold a candle up to trust, and shine my light for others to see what's possible.

Daily Journal - Day 106 / 260

Today is _____ / _____ / _____

My Gratitudes:

1. _____

2. _____

3. _____

My Gratitude Intentions - Setting my GPS / SAT NAV:

1. _____

2. _____

3. _____

Journaling. Happy Stuff. Photos. (Or extra Gratitude!)

Daily Journal - Day 107 / 259

Today is _____ / _____ / _____

My Gratitudes:

1. _____

2. _____

3. _____

My Gratitude Intentions - Setting my GPS / SAT NAV:

1. _____

2. _____

3. _____

Journaling. Happy Stuff. Photos. (Or extra Gratitude!)

Daily Journal - Day 108 / 258

Today is _____ / _____ / _____

My Gratitudes:

1. _____

2. _____

3. _____

My Gratitude Intentions - Setting my GPS / SAT NAV:

1. _____

2. _____

3. _____

Journaling. Happy Stuff. Photos. (Or extra Gratitude!)

Daily Journal - Day 109 / 257

Today is _____ / _____ / _____

My Gratitudes:

1. _____

2. _____

3. _____

My Gratitude Intentions - Setting my GPS / SAT NAV:

1. _____

2. _____

3. _____

Journaling. Happy Stuff. Photos. (Or extra Gratitude!)

Daily Journal - Day 110 / 256

Today is _____ / _____ / _____

My Gratitudes:

1. _____

2. _____

3. _____

My Gratitude Intentions - Setting my GPS / SAT NAV:

1. _____

2. _____

3. _____

Journaling. Happy Stuff. Photos. (Or extra Gratitude!)

Daily Journal - Day 111 / 255

Today is _____ / _____ / _____

My Gratitudes:

1. _____

2. _____

3. _____

My Gratitude Intentions - Setting my GPS / SAT NAV:

1. _____

2. _____

3. _____

Journaling. Happy Stuff. Photos. (Or extra Gratitude!)

Daily Journal - Day 112 / 254

Today is _____ / _____ / _____

My Gratitudes:

1. _____

2. _____

3. _____

My Gratitude Intentions - Setting my GPS / SAT NAV:

1. _____

2. _____

3. _____

Journaling. Happy Stuff. Photos. (Or extra Gratitude!)

Sometimes humble submission holds the key to peace.
The work falls away and simplicity reigns.

Daily Journal - Day 113 / 253

Today is _____ / _____ / _____

My Gratitudes:

1. _____

2. _____

3. _____

My Gratitude Intentions - Setting my GPS / SAT NAV:

1. _____

2. _____

3. _____

Journaling. Happy Stuff. Photos. (Or extra Gratitude!)

Daily Journal - Day 114 / 252

Today is _____ / _____ / _____

My Gratitudes:

1. _____

2. _____

3. _____

My Gratitude Intentions - Setting my GPS / SAT NAV:

1. _____

2. _____

3. _____

Journaling. Happy Stuff. Photos. (Or extra Gratitude!)

Daily Journal - Day 115 / 251

Today is _____ / _____ / _____

My Gratitudes:

1. _____

2. _____

3. _____

My Gratitude Intentions - Setting my GPS / SAT NAV:

1. _____

2. _____

3. _____

Journaling. Happy Stuff. Photos. (Or extra Gratitude!)

Daily Journal - Day 116 / 250

Today is _____ / _____ / _____

My Gratitudes:

1. _____

2. _____

3. _____

My Gratitude Intentions - Setting my GPS / SAT NAV:

1. _____

2. _____

3. _____

Journaling. Happy Stuff. Photos. (Or extra Gratitude!)

Daily Journal - Day 117 / 249

Today is _____ / _____ / _____

My Gratitudes:

1. _____

2. _____

3. _____

My Gratitude Intentions - Setting my GPS / SAT NAV:

1. _____

2. _____

3. _____

Journaling. Happy Stuff. Photos. (Or extra Gratitude!)

Daily Journal - Day 118 / 248

Today is _____ / _____ / _____

My Gratitudes:

1. _____

2. _____

3. _____

My Gratitude Intentions - Setting my GPS / SAT NAV:

1. _____

2. _____

3. _____

Journaling. Happy Stuff. Photos. (Or extra Gratitude!)

Acceptance is the prerequisite to healthy action. It is the starting block from which we spring forward into endless opportunity and abundant living.

Daily Journal - Day 119 / 247

Today is _____ / _____ / _____

My Gratitudes:

1. _____

2. _____

3. _____

My Gratitude Intentions - Setting my GPS / SAT NAV:

1. _____

2. _____

3. _____

Journaling. Happy Stuff. Photos. (Or extra Gratitude!)

Daily Journal - Day 120 / 246

Today is _____ / _____ / _____

My Gratitudes:

1. _____

2. _____

3. _____

My Gratitude Intentions - Setting my GPS / SAT NAV:

1. _____

2. _____

3. _____

Journaling. Happy Stuff. Photos. (Or extra Gratitude!)

Daily Journal - Day 121 / 245

Today is _____ / _____ / _____

My Gratitudes:

1. _____

2. _____

3. _____

My Gratitude Intentions - Setting my GPS / SAT NAV:

1. _____

2. _____

3. _____

Journaling. Happy Stuff. Photos. (Or extra Gratitude!)

Daily Journal - Day 122 / 244

Today is _____ / _____ / _____

My Gratitudes:

1. _____

2. _____

3. _____

My Gratitude Intentions - Setting my GPS / SAT NAV:

1. _____

2. _____

3. _____

Journaling. Happy Stuff. Photos. (Or extra Gratitude!)

Daily Journal - Day 123 / 243

Today is _____ / _____ / _____

My Gratitudes:

1. _____

2. _____

3. _____

My Gratitude Intentions - Setting my GPS / SAT NAV:

1. _____

2. _____

3. _____

Journaling. Happy Stuff. Photos. (Or extra Gratitude!)

Daily Journal - Day 124 / 242

Today is _____ / _____ / _____

My Gratitudes:

1. _____

2. _____

3. _____

My Gratitude Intentions - Setting my GPS / SAT NAV:

1. _____

2. _____

3. _____

Journaling. Happy Stuff. Photos. (Or extra Gratitude!)

Freedom comes when I know that discipline is the gem of happiness, resting majestically in the crown of balance and effortless living.

Daily Journal - Day 125 / 241

Today is _____ / _____ / _____

My Gratitudes:

1. _____

2. _____

3. _____

My Gratitude Intentions - Setting my GPS / SAT NAV:

1. _____

2. _____

3. _____

Journaling. Happy Stuff. Photos. (Or extra Gratitude!)

Daily Journal - Day 126 / 240

Today is _____ / _____ / _____

My Gratitudes:

1. _____

2. _____

3. _____

My Gratitude Intentions - Setting my GPS / SAT NAV:

1. _____

2. _____

3. _____

Journaling. Happy Stuff. Photos. (Or extra Gratitude!)

Daily Journal - Day 127 / 239

Today is _____ / _____ / _____

My Gratitudes:

1. _____

2. _____

3. _____

My Gratitude Intentions - Setting my GPS / SAT NAV:

1. _____

2. _____

3. _____

Journaling. Happy Stuff. Photos. (Or extra Gratitude!)

Daily Journal - Day 128 / 238

Today is _____ / _____ / _____

My Gratitudes:

1. _____

2. _____

3. _____

My Gratitude Intentions - Setting my GPS / SAT NAV:

1. _____

2. _____

3. _____

Journaling. Happy Stuff. Photos. (Or extra Gratitude!)

Daily Journal - Day 129 / 237

Today is _____ / _____ / _____

My Gratitudes:

1. _____

2. _____

3. _____

My Gratitude Intentions - Setting my GPS / SAT NAV:

1. _____

2. _____

3. _____

Journaling. Happy Stuff. Photos. (Or extra Gratitude!)

Daily Journal - Day 130 / 236

Today is _____ / _____ / _____

My Gratitudes:

1. _____

2. _____

3. _____

My Gratitude Intentions - Setting my GPS / SAT NAV:

1. _____

2. _____

3. _____

Journaling. Happy Stuff. Photos. (Or extra Gratitude!)

Like the soft white feather floating gently down, serenity lands quietly upon my soul when I create the space for it in my life.

Daily Journal - Day 131 / 235

Today is _____ / _____ / _____

My Gratitudes:

1. _____

2. _____

3. _____

My Gratitude Intentions - Setting my GPS / SAT NAV:

1. _____

2. _____

3. _____

Journaling. Happy Stuff. Photos. (Or extra Gratitude!)

Daily Journal - Day 132 / 234

Today is _____ / _____ / _____

My Gratitudes:

1. _____

2. _____

3. _____

My Gratitude Intentions - Setting my GPS / SAT NAV:

1. _____

2. _____

3. _____

Journaling. Happy Stuff. Photos. (Or extra Gratitude!)

Daily Journal - Day 133 / 233

Today is _____ / _____ / _____

My Gratitudes:

1. _____

2. _____

3. _____

My Gratitude Intentions - Setting my GPS / SAT NAV:

1. _____

2. _____

3. _____

Journaling. Happy Stuff. Photos. (Or extra Gratitude!)

Daily Journal - Day 134 / 232

Today is _____ / _____ / _____

My Gratitudes:

1. _____

2. _____

3. _____

My Gratitude Intentions - Setting my GPS / SAT NAV:

1. _____

2. _____

3. _____

Journaling. Happy Stuff. Photos. (Or extra Gratitude!)

Daily Journal - Day 135 / 231

Today is _____ / _____ / _____

My Gratitudes:

1. _____

2. _____

3. _____

My Gratitude Intentions - Setting my GPS / SAT NAV:

1. _____

2. _____

3. _____

Journaling. Happy Stuff. Photos. (Or extra Gratitude!)

Daily Journal - Day 136 / 230

Today is _____ / _____ / _____

My Gratitudes:

1. _____

2. _____

3. _____

My Gratitude Intentions - Setting my GPS / SAT NAV:

1. _____

2. _____

3. _____

Journaling. Happy Stuff. Photos. (Or extra Gratitude!)

Living for giving inspires my heart and excites my life juices, especially when I know that the purest form of giving must always be to myself first.

Daily Journal - Day 137 / 229

Today is _____ / _____ / _____

My Gratitudes:

1. _____

2. _____

3. _____

My Gratitude Intentions - Setting my GPS / SAT NAV:

1. _____

2. _____

3. _____

Journaling. Happy Stuff. Photos. (Or extra Gratitude!)

Daily Journal - Day 138 / 228

Today is _____ / _____ / _____

My Gratitudes:

1. _____

2. _____

3. _____

My Gratitude Intentions - Setting my GPS / SAT NAV:

1. _____

2. _____

3. _____

Journaling. Happy Stuff. Photos. (Or extra Gratitude!)

Daily Journal - Day 139 / 227

Today is _____ / _____ / _____

My Gratitudes:

1. _____

2. _____

3. _____

My Gratitude Intentions - Setting my GPS / SAT NAV:

1. _____

2. _____

3. _____

Journaling. Happy Stuff. Photos. (Or extra Gratitude!)

Daily Journal - Day 140 / 226

Today is _____ / _____ / _____

My Gratitudes:

1. _____

2. _____

3. _____

My Gratitude Intentions - Setting my GPS / SAT NAV:

1. _____

2. _____

3. _____

Journaling. Happy Stuff. Photos. (Or extra Gratitude!)

Daily Journal - Day 141 / 225

Today is _____ / _____ / _____

My Gratitudes:

1. _____

2. _____

3. _____

My Gratitude Intentions - Setting my GPS / SAT NAV:

1. _____

2. _____

3. _____

Journaling. Happy Stuff. Photos. (Or extra Gratitude!)

Daily Journal - Day 142 / 224

Today is _____ / _____ / _____

My Gratitudes:

1. _____

2. _____

3. _____

My Gratitude Intentions - Setting my GPS / SAT NAV:

1. _____

2. _____

3. _____

Journaling. Happy Stuff. Photos. (Or extra Gratitude!)

When I explore the expanding reaches of my human potential under the light of my own forgiveness, my heart and soul delight in the revelation of my endless possibilities.

Daily Journal - Day 143 / 223

Today is _____ / _____ / _____

My Gratitudes:

1. _____

2. _____

3. _____

My Gratitude Intentions - Setting my GPS / SAT NAV:

1. _____

2. _____

3. _____

Journaling. Happy Stuff. Photos. (Or extra Gratitude!)

Daily Journal - Day 144 / 222

Today is _____ / _____ / _____

My Gratitudes:

1. _____

2. _____

3. _____

My Gratitude Intentions - Setting my GPS / SAT NAV:

1. _____

2. _____

3. _____

Journaling. Happy Stuff. Photos. (Or extra Gratitude!)

Daily Journal - Day 145 / 221

Today is _____ / _____ / _____

My Gratitudes:

1. _____

2. _____

3. _____

My Gratitude Intentions - Setting my GPS / SAT NAV:

1. _____

2. _____

3. _____

Journaling. Happy Stuff. Photos. (Or extra Gratitude!)

Daily Journal - Day 146 / 220

Today is _____ / _____ / _____

My Gratitudes:

1. _____

2. _____

3. _____

My Gratitude Intentions - Setting my GPS / SAT NAV:

1. _____

2. _____

3. _____

Journaling. Happy Stuff. Photos. (Or extra Gratitude!)

Daily Journal - Day 147 / 219

Today is _____ / _____ / _____

My Gratitudes:

1. _____

2. _____

3. _____

My Gratitude Intentions - Setting my GPS / SAT NAV:

1. _____

2. _____

3. _____

Journaling. Happy Stuff. Photos. (Or extra Gratitude!)

Daily Journal - Day 148 / 218

Today is _____ / _____ / _____

My Gratitudes:

1. _____

2. _____

3. _____

My Gratitude Intentions - Setting my GPS / SAT NAV:

1. _____

2. _____

3. _____

Journaling. Happy Stuff. Photos. (Or extra Gratitude!)

When I ask for what I need and practice trusting, the reward for
my saturated soul is the delight of a truly peaceful life.

Daily Journal - Day 149 / 217

Today is _____ / _____ / _____

My Gratitudes:

1. _____

2. _____

3. _____

My Gratitude Intentions - Setting my GPS / SAT NAV:

1. _____

2. _____

3. _____

Journaling. Happy Stuff. Photos. (Or extra Gratitude!)

Daily Journal - Day 150 / 216

Today is _____ / _____ / _____

My Gratitudes:

1. _____

2. _____

3. _____

My Gratitude Intentions - Setting my GPS / SAT NAV:

1. _____

2. _____

3. _____

Journaling. Happy Stuff. Photos. (Or extra Gratitude!)

Daily Journal - Day 151 / 215

Today is _____ / _____ / _____

My Gratitudes:

1. _____

2. _____

3. _____

My Gratitude Intentions - Setting my GPS / SAT NAV:

1. _____

2. _____

3. _____

Journaling. Happy Stuff. Photos. (Or extra Gratitude!)

Daily Journal - Day 152 / 214

Today is _____ / _____ / _____

My Gratitudes:

1. _____

2. _____

3. _____

My Gratitude Intentions - Setting my GPS / SAT NAV:

1. _____

2. _____

3. _____

Journaling. Happy Stuff. Photos. (Or extra Gratitude!)

Daily Journal - Day 153 / 213

Today is _____ / _____ / _____

My Gratitudes:

1. _____

2. _____

3. _____

My Gratitude Intentions - Setting my GPS / SAT NAV:

1. _____

2. _____

3. _____

Journaling. Happy Stuff. Photos. (Or extra Gratitude!)

Daily Journal - Day 154 / 212

Today is _____ / _____ / _____

My Gratitudes:

1. _____

2. _____

3. _____

My Gratitude Intentions - Setting my GPS / SAT NAV:

1. _____

2. _____

3. _____

Journaling. Happy Stuff. Photos. (Or extra Gratitude!)

True communion and connection are life skills at my disposal when I practice reaching out to even one other human being. Good life comes from the opportunities I take responsibility for creating.

Daily Journal - Day 155 / 211

Today is _____ / _____ / _____

My Gratitudes:

1. _____

2. _____

3. _____

My Gratitude Intentions - Setting my GPS / SAT NAV:

1. _____

2. _____

3. _____

Journaling. Happy Stuff. Photos. (Or extra Gratitude!)

Daily Journal - Day 156 / 210

Today is _____ / _____ / _____

My Gratitudes:

1. _____

2. _____

3. _____

My Gratitude Intentions - Setting my GPS / SAT NAV:

1. _____

2. _____

3. _____

Journaling. Happy Stuff. Photos. (Or extra Gratitude!)

Daily Journal - Day 157 / 209

Today is _____ / _____ / _____

My Gratitudes:

1. _____

2. _____

3. _____

My Gratitude Intentions - Setting my GPS / SAT NAV:

1. _____

2. _____

3. _____

Journaling. Happy Stuff. Photos. (Or extra Gratitude!)

Daily Journal - Day 158 / 208

Today is _____ / _____ / _____

My Gratitudes:

1. _____

2. _____

3. _____

My Gratitude Intentions - Setting my GPS / SAT NAV:

1. _____

2. _____

3. _____

Journaling. Happy Stuff. Photos. (Or extra Gratitude!)

Daily Journal - Day 159 / 207

Today is _____ / _____ / _____

My Gratitudes:

1. _____

2. _____

3. _____

My Gratitude Intentions - Setting my GPS / SAT NAV:

1. _____

2. _____

3. _____

Journaling. Happy Stuff. Photos. (Or extra Gratitude!)

Daily Journal - Day 160 / 206

Today is _____ / _____ / _____

My Gratitudes:

1. _____

2. _____

3. _____

My Gratitude Intentions - Setting my GPS / SAT NAV:

1. _____

2. _____

3. _____

Journaling. Happy Stuff. Photos. (Or extra Gratitude!)

Happiness lands on my life when I see the light through the
dark forest and believe that it is there also.

Daily Journal - Day 161 / 205

Today is _____ / _____ / _____

My Gratitudes:

1. _____

2. _____

3. _____

My Gratitude Intentions - Setting my GPS / SAT NAV:

1. _____

2. _____

3. _____

Journaling. Happy Stuff. Photos. (Or extra Gratitude!)

Daily Journal - Day 162 / 204

Today is _____ / _____ / _____

My Gratitudes:

1. _____

2. _____

3. _____

My Gratitude Intentions - Setting my GPS / SAT NAV:

1. _____

2. _____

3. _____

Journaling. Happy Stuff. Photos. (Or extra Gratitude!)

Daily Journal - Day 163 / 203

Today is _____ / _____ / _____

My Gratitudes:

1. _____

2. _____

3. _____

My Gratitude Intentions - Setting my GPS / SAT NAV:

1. _____

2. _____

3. _____

Journaling. Happy Stuff. Photos. (Or extra Gratitude!)

Daily Journal - Day 164 / 202

Today is _____ / _____ / _____

My Gratitudes:

1. _____

2. _____

3. _____

My Gratitude Intentions - Setting my GPS / SAT NAV:

1. _____

2. _____

3. _____

Journaling. Happy Stuff. Photos. (Or extra Gratitude!)

Daily Journal - Day 165 / 201

Today is _____ / _____ / _____

My Gratitudes:

1. _____

2. _____

3. _____

My Gratitude Intentions - Setting my GPS / SAT NAV:

1. _____

2. _____

3. _____

Journaling. Happy Stuff. Photos. (Or extra Gratitude!)

Daily Journal - Day 166 / 200

Today is _____ / _____ / _____

My Gratitudes:

1. _____

2. _____

3. _____

My Gratitude Intentions - Setting my GPS / SAT NAV:

1. _____

2. _____

3. _____

Journaling. Happy Stuff. Photos. (Or extra Gratitude!)

Mother nature is the access to the kingdom
of abundance where lives the heart of the spiritual.

Daily Journal - Day 167 / 199

Today is _____ / _____ / _____

My Gratitudes:

1. _____

2. _____

3. _____

My Gratitude Intentions - Setting my GPS / SAT NAV:

1. _____

2. _____

3. _____

Journaling. Happy Stuff. Photos. (Or extra Gratitude!)

Daily Journal - Day 168 / 198

Today is _____ / _____ / _____

My Gratitudes:

1. _____

2. _____

3. _____

My Gratitude Intentions - Setting my GPS / SAT NAV:

1. _____

2. _____

3. _____

Journaling. Happy Stuff. Photos. (Or extra Gratitude!)

Daily Journal - Day 169 / 197

Today is _____ / _____ / _____

My Gratitudes:

1. _____

2. _____

3. _____

My Gratitude Intentions - Setting my GPS / SAT NAV:

1. _____

2. _____

3. _____

Journaling. Happy Stuff. Photos. (Or extra Gratitude!)

Daily Journal - Day 170 / 196

Today is _____ / _____ / _____

My Gratitudes:

1. _____

2. _____

3. _____

My Gratitude Intentions - Setting my GPS / SAT NAV:

1. _____

2. _____

3. _____

Journaling. Happy Stuff. Photos. (Or extra Gratitude!)

Daily Journal - Day 171 / 195

Today is _____ / _____ / _____

My Gratitudes:

1. _____

2. _____

3. _____

My Gratitude Intentions - Setting my GPS / SAT NAV:

1. _____

2. _____

3. _____

Journaling. Happy Stuff. Photos. (Or extra Gratitude!)

Daily Journal - Day 172 / 194

Today is _____ / _____ / _____

My Gratitudes:

1. _____

2. _____

3. _____

My Gratitude Intentions - Setting my GPS / SAT NAV:

1. _____

2. _____

3. _____

Journaling. Happy Stuff. Photos. (Or extra Gratitude!)

Doing it more often is what will render my life manageable, joyous and free.

Daily Journal - Day 173 / 193

Today is _____ /_____ /_____

My Gratitudes:

1. _____

2. _____

3. _____

My Gratitude Intentions - Setting my GPS / SAT NAV:

1. _____

2. _____

3. _____

Journaling. Happy Stuff. Photos. (Or extra Gratitude!)

Daily Journal - Day 174 / 192

Today is _____ / _____ / _____

My Gratitudes:

1. _____

2. _____

3. _____

My Gratitude Intentions - Setting my GPS / SAT NAV:

1. _____

2. _____

3. _____

Journaling. Happy Stuff. Photos. (Or extra Gratitude!)

Daily Journal - Day 175 / 191

Today is _____ / _____ / _____

My Gratitudes:

1. _____

2. _____

3. _____

My Gratitude Intentions - Setting my GPS / SAT NAV:

1. _____

2. _____

3. _____

Journaling. Happy Stuff. Photos. (Or extra Gratitude!)

Daily Journal - Day 176 / 190

Today is _____ / _____ / _____

My Gratitudes:

1. _____

2. _____

3. _____

My Gratitude Intentions - Setting my GPS / SAT NAV:

1. _____

2. _____

3. _____

Journaling. Happy Stuff. Photos. (Or extra Gratitude!)

Daily Journal - Day 177 / 189

Today is _____ / _____ / _____

My Gratitudes:

1. _____

2. _____

3. _____

My Gratitude Intentions - Setting my GPS / SAT NAV:

1. _____

2. _____

3. _____

Journaling. Happy Stuff. Photos. (Or extra Gratitude!)

Daily Journal - Day 178 / 188

Today is _____ / _____ / _____

My Gratitudes:

1. _____

2. _____

3. _____

My Gratitude Intentions - Setting my GPS / SAT NAV:

1. _____

2. _____

3. _____

Journaling. Happy Stuff. Photos. (Or extra Gratitude!)

Life is a manifestation of all that is possible and all that will find its way to you if you believe it.

Daily Journal - Day 179 / 187

Today is _____ / _____ / _____

My Gratitudes:

1. _____

2. _____

3. _____

My Gratitude Intentions - Setting my GPS / SAT NAV:

1. _____

2. _____

3. _____

Journaling. Happy Stuff. Photos. (Or extra Gratitude!)

Daily Journal - Day 180 / 186

Today is _____ / _____ / _____

My Gratitudes:

1. _____

2. _____

3. _____

My Gratitude Intentions - Setting my GPS / SAT NAV:

1. _____

2. _____

3. _____

Journaling. Happy Stuff. Photos. (Or extra Gratitude!)

Daily Journal - Day 181 / 185

Today is _____ /_____ /_____

My Gratitudes:

1. _____

2. _____

3. _____

My Gratitude Intentions - Setting my GPS / SAT NAV:

1. _____

2. _____

3. _____

Journaling. Happy Stuff. Photos. (Or extra Gratitude!)

Daily Journal - Day 182 / 184

Today is _____ / _____ / _____

My Gratitudes:

1. _____

2. _____

3. _____

My Gratitude Intentions - Setting my GPS / SAT NAV:

1. _____

2. _____

3. _____

Journaling. Happy Stuff. Photos. (Or extra Gratitude!)

Daily Journal - Day 183 / 183

Today is _____ / _____ / _____

My Gratitudes:

1. _____

2. _____

3. _____

My Gratitude Intentions - Setting my GPS / SAT NAV:

1. _____

2. _____

3. _____

Journaling. Happy Stuff. Photos. (Or extra Gratitude!)

Daily Journal - Day 184 / 182

Today is _____ / _____ / _____

My Gratitudes:

1. _____

2. _____

3. _____

My Gratitude Intentions - Setting my GPS / SAT NAV:

1. _____

2. _____

3. _____

Journaling. Happy Stuff. Photos. (Or extra Gratitude!)

Serenity is the way of being for those who want the peace
of life to live deep in their souls.

Daily Journal - Day 185 / 181

Today is _____ /_____ /_____

My Gratitudes:

1. _____

2. _____

3. _____

My Gratitude Intentions - Setting my GPS / SAT NAV:

1. _____

2. _____

3. _____

Journaling. Happy Stuff. Photos. (Or extra Gratitude!)

Daily Journal - Day 186 / 180

Today is _____ / _____ / _____

My Gratitudes:

1. _____

2. _____

3. _____

My Gratitude Intentions - Setting my GPS / SAT NAV:

1. _____

2. _____

3. _____

Journaling. Happy Stuff. Photos. (Or extra Gratitude!)

Daily Journal - Day 187 / 179

Today is _____ /_____ /_____

My Gratitudes:

1. _____

2. _____

3. _____

My Gratitude Intentions - Setting my GPS / SAT NAV:

1. _____

2. _____

3. _____

Journaling. Happy Stuff. Photos. (Or extra Gratitude!)

Daily Journal - Day 188 / 178

Today is _____ / _____ / _____

My Gratitudes:

1. _____

2. _____

3. _____

My Gratitude Intentions - Setting my GPS / SAT NAV:

1. _____

2. _____

3. _____

Journaling. Happy Stuff. Photos. (Or extra Gratitude!)

Daily Journal - Day 189 / 177

Today is _____ /_____ /_____

My Gratitudes:

1. _____

2. _____

3. _____

My Gratitude Intentions - Setting my GPS / SAT NAV:

1. _____

2. _____

3. _____

Journaling. Happy Stuff. Photos. (Or extra Gratitude!)

Daily Journal - Day 190 / 176

Today is _____ / _____ / _____

My Gratitudes:

1. _____

2. _____

3. _____

My Gratitude Intentions - Setting my GPS / SAT NAV:

1. _____

2. _____

3. _____

Journaling. Happy Stuff. Photos. (Or extra Gratitude!)

Clarity is an exciting state I can get to when I make the decision to
let go of my old ways of thinking.

Daily Journal - Day 191 / 175

Today is _____ / _____ / _____

My Gratitudes:

1. _____

2. _____

3. _____

My Gratitude Intentions - Setting my GPS / SAT NAV:

1. _____

2. _____

3. _____

Journaling. Happy Stuff. Photos. (Or extra Gratitude!)

Daily Journal - Day 192 / 174

Today is _____ / _____ / _____

My Gratitudes:

1. _____

2. _____

3. _____

My Gratitude Intentions - Setting my GPS / SAT NAV:

1. _____

2. _____

3. _____

Journaling. Happy Stuff. Photos. (Or extra Gratitude!)

Daily Journal - Day 193 / 173

Today is _____ /_____ /_____

My Gratitudes:

1. _____

2. _____

3. _____

My Gratitude Intentions - Setting my GPS / SAT NAV:

1. _____

2. _____

3. _____

Journaling. Happy Stuff. Photos. (Or extra Gratitude!)

Daily Journal - Day 194 / 172

Today is _____ / _____ / _____

My Gratitudes:

1. _____

2. _____

3. _____

My Gratitude Intentions - Setting my GPS / SAT NAV:

1. _____

2. _____

3. _____

Journaling. Happy Stuff. Photos. (Or extra Gratitude!)

Daily Journal - Day 195 / 171

Today is _____ / _____ / _____

My Gratitudes:

1. _____

2. _____

3. _____

My Gratitude Intentions - Setting my GPS / SAT NAV:

1. _____

2. _____

3. _____

Journaling. Happy Stuff. Photos. (Or extra Gratitude!)

Daily Journal - Day 196 / 170

Today is _____ / _____ / _____

My Gratitudes:

1. _____

2. _____

3. _____

My Gratitude Intentions - Setting my GPS / SAT NAV:

1. _____

2. _____

3. _____

Journaling. Happy Stuff. Photos. (Or extra Gratitude!)

Focusing on all that is good in my life grounds me in positivity.

Daily Journal - Day 197 / 169

Today is _____ / _____ / _____

My Gratitudes:

1. _____

2. _____

3. _____

My Gratitude Intentions - Setting my GPS / SAT NAV:

1. _____

2. _____

3. _____

Journaling. Happy Stuff. Photos. (Or extra Gratitude!)

Daily Journal - Day 198 / 168

Today is _____ / _____ / _____

My Gratitudes:

1. _____

2. _____

3. _____

My Gratitude Intentions - Setting my GPS / SAT NAV:

1. _____

2. _____

3. _____

Journaling. Happy Stuff. Photos. (Or extra Gratitude!)

Daily Journal - Day 199 / 167

Today is _____ / _____ / _____

My Gratitudes:

1. _____

2. _____

3. _____

My Gratitude Intentions - Setting my GPS / SAT NAV:

1. _____

2. _____

3. _____

Journaling. Happy Stuff. Photos. (Or extra Gratitude!)

Daily Journal - Day 200 / 166

Today is _____ / _____ / _____

My Gratitudes:

1. _____

2. _____

3. _____

My Gratitude Intentions - Setting my GPS / SAT NAV:

1. _____

2. _____

3. _____

Journaling. Happy Stuff. Photos. (Or extra Gratitude!)

Daily Journal - Day 201 / 165

Today is _____ / _____ / _____

My Gratitudes:

1. _____

2. _____

3. _____

My Gratitude Intentions - Setting my GPS / SAT NAV:

1. _____

2. _____

3. _____

Journaling. Happy Stuff. Photos. (Or extra Gratitude!)

Daily Journal - Day 202 / 164

Today is _____ / _____ / _____

My Gratitudes:

1. _____

2. _____

3. _____

My Gratitude Intentions - Setting my GPS / SAT NAV:

1. _____

2. _____

3. _____

Journaling. Happy Stuff. Photos. (Or extra Gratitude!)

The challenge is to trust through the darkness, to know for
sure that the highest caliber of confidence can only come there.

Daily Journal - Day 203 / 163

Today is _____ / _____ / _____

My Gratitudes:

1. _____

2. _____

3. _____

My Gratitude Intentions - Setting my GPS / SAT NAV:

1. _____

2. _____

3. _____

Journaling. Happy Stuff. Photos. (Or extra Gratitude!)

Daily Journal - Day 204 / 162

Today is _____ / _____ / _____

My Gratitudes:

1. _____

2. _____

3. _____

My Gratitude Intentions - Setting my GPS / SAT NAV:

1. _____

2. _____

3. _____

Journaling. Happy Stuff. Photos. (Or extra Gratitude!)

Daily Journal - Day 205 / 161

Today is _____ / _____ / _____

My Gratitudes:

1. _____

2. _____

3. _____

My Gratitude Intentions - Setting my GPS / SAT NAV:

1. _____

2. _____

3. _____

Journaling. Happy Stuff. Photos. (Or extra Gratitude!)

Daily Journal - Day 206 / 160

Today is _____ /_____ /_____

My Gratitudes:

1. _____

2. _____

3. _____

My Gratitude Intentions - Setting my GPS / SAT NAV:

1. _____

2. _____

3. _____

Journaling. Happy Stuff. Photos. (Or extra Gratitude!)

Daily Journal - Day 207 / 159

Today is _____ / _____ / _____

My Gratitudes:

1. _____

2. _____

3. _____

My Gratitude Intentions - Setting my GPS / SAT NAV:

1. _____

2. _____

3. _____

Journaling. Happy Stuff. Photos. (Or extra Gratitude!)

Daily Journal - Day 208 / 158

Today is _____ / _____ / _____

My Gratitudes:

1. _____

2. _____

3. _____

My Gratitude Intentions - Setting my GPS / SAT NAV:

1. _____

2. _____

3. _____

Journaling. Happy Stuff. Photos. (Or extra Gratitude!)

So I close my eyes and see the light of gratitude coming through my body powered by my healthy belief and charged by my connection to our universe.

Daily Journal - Day 209 / 157

Today is _____ / _____ / _____

My Gratitudes:

1. _____

2. _____

3. _____

My Gratitude Intentions - Setting my GPS / SAT NAV:

1. _____

2. _____

3. _____

Journaling. Happy Stuff. Photos. (Or extra Gratitude!)

Daily Journal - Day 210 / 156

Today is _____ / _____ / _____

My Gratitudes:

1. _____

2. _____

3. _____

My Gratitude Intentions - Setting my GPS / SAT NAV:

1. _____

2. _____

3. _____

Journaling. Happy Stuff. Photos. (Or extra Gratitude!)

Daily Journal - Day 211 / 155

Today is _____ / _____ / _____

My Gratitudes:

1. _____

2. _____

3. _____

My Gratitude Intentions - Setting my GPS / SAT NAV:

1. _____

2. _____

3. _____

Journaling. Happy Stuff. Photos. (Or extra Gratitude!)

Daily Journal - Day 212 / 154

Today is _____ / _____ / _____

My Gratitudes:

1. _____

2. _____

3. _____

My Gratitude Intentions - Setting my GPS / SAT NAV:

1. _____

2. _____

3. _____

Journaling. Happy Stuff. Photos. (Or extra Gratitude!)

Daily Journal - Day 213 / 153

Today is _____ / _____ / _____

My Gratitudes:

1. _____

2. _____

3. _____

My Gratitude Intentions - Setting my GPS / SAT NAV:

1. _____

2. _____

3. _____

Journaling. Happy Stuff. Photos. (Or extra Gratitude!)

Daily Journal - Day 214 / 152

Today is _____ / _____ / _____

My Gratitudes:

1. _____

2. _____

3. _____

My Gratitude Intentions - Setting my GPS / SAT NAV:

1. _____

2. _____

3. _____

Journaling. Happy Stuff. Photos. (Or extra Gratitude!)

Below the surface of the outer world of my being the Power Centre organizes my life, challenges me to step out, protects me at all times with the ancient wisdom that is the Source.

Daily Journal - Day 215 / 151

Today is _____ / _____ / _____

My Gratitudes:

1. _____

2. _____

3. _____

My Gratitude Intentions - Setting my GPS / SAT NAV:

1. _____

2. _____

3. _____

Journaling. Happy Stuff. Photos. (Or extra Gratitude!)

Daily Journal - Day 216 / 150

Today is _____ / _____ / _____

My Gratitudes:

1. _____

2. _____

3. _____

My Gratitude Intentions - Setting my GPS / SAT NAV:

1. _____

2. _____

3. _____

Journaling. Happy Stuff. Photos. (Or extra Gratitude!)

Daily Journal - Day 217 / 149

Today is _____ / _____ / _____

My Gratitudes:

1. _____

2. _____

3. _____

My Gratitude Intentions - Setting my GPS / SAT NAV:

1. _____

2. _____

3. _____

Journaling. Happy Stuff. Photos. (Or extra Gratitude!)

Daily Journal - Day 218 / 148

Today is _____ / _____ / _____

My Gratitudes:

1. _____

2. _____

3. _____

My Gratitude Intentions - Setting my GPS / SAT NAV:

1. _____

2. _____

3. _____

Journaling. Happy Stuff. Photos. (Or extra Gratitude!)

Daily Journal - Day 219 / 147

Today is _____ / _____ / _____

My Gratitudes:

1. _____

2. _____

3. _____

My Gratitude Intentions - Setting my GPS / SAT NAV:

1. _____

2. _____

3. _____

Journaling. Happy Stuff. Photos. (Or extra Gratitude!)

Daily Journal - Day 220 / 146

Today is _____ / _____ / _____

My Gratitudes:

1. _____

2. _____

3. _____

My Gratitude Intentions - Setting my GPS / SAT NAV:

1. _____

2. _____

3. _____

Journaling. Happy Stuff. Photos. (Or extra Gratitude!)

Along the hub of being lies the Source of Energy, which drives and moves me. Peering inside this, with the delight of an enthused child lights up my life, and brings me into the magical world of endless possibility.

Daily Journal - Day 221 / 145

Today is _____ / _____ / _____

My Gratitudes:

1. _____

2. _____

3. _____

My Gratitude Intentions - Setting my GPS / SAT NAV:

1. _____

2. _____

3. _____

Journaling. Happy Stuff. Photos. (Or extra Gratitude!)

Daily Journal - Day 222 / 144

Today is _____ /_____ /_____

My Gratitudes:

1. _____

2. _____

3. _____

My Gratitude Intentions - Setting my GPS / SAT NAV:

1. _____

2. _____

3. _____

Journaling. Happy Stuff. Photos. (Or extra Gratitude!)

Daily Journal - Day 223 / 143

Today is _____ / _____ / _____

My Gratitudes:

1. _____

2. _____

3. _____

My Gratitude Intentions - Setting my GPS / SAT NAV:

1. _____

2. _____

3. _____

Journaling. Happy Stuff. Photos. (Or extra Gratitude!)

Daily Journal - Day 224 / 142

Today is _____ / _____ / _____

My Gratitudes:

1. _____

2. _____

3. _____

My Gratitude Intentions - Setting my GPS / SAT NAV:

1. _____

2. _____

3. _____

Journaling. Happy Stuff. Photos. (Or extra Gratitude!)

Daily Journal - Day 225 / 141

Today is _____ / _____ / _____

My Gratitudes:

1. _____

2. _____

3. _____

My Gratitude Intentions - Setting my GPS / SAT NAV:

1. _____

2. _____

3. _____

Journaling. Happy Stuff. Photos. (Or extra Gratitude!)

Daily Journal - Day 226 / 140

Today is _____ / _____ / _____

My Gratitudes:

1. _____

2. _____

3. _____

My Gratitude Intentions - Setting my GPS / SAT NAV:

1. _____

2. _____

3. _____

Journaling. Happy Stuff. Photos. (Or extra Gratitude!)

Getting past my past sets me free to indulge in the abundance of the world I live in and crank up the joy big time!

Daily Journal - Day 227 / 139

Today is _____ / _____ / _____

My Gratitudes:

1. _____

2. _____

3. _____

My Gratitude Intentions - Setting my GPS / SAT NAV:

1. _____

2. _____

3. _____

Journaling. Happy Stuff. Photos. (Or extra Gratitude!)

Daily Journal - Day 228 / 138

Today is _____ /_____ /_____

My Gratitudes:

1. _____

2. _____

3. _____

My Gratitude Intentions - Setting my GPS / SAT NAV:

1. _____

2. _____

3. _____

Journaling. Happy Stuff. Photos. (Or extra Gratitude!)

Daily Journal - Day 229 / 137

Today is _____ / _____ / _____

My Gratitudes:

1. _____

2. _____

3. _____

My Gratitude Intentions - Setting my GPS / SAT NAV:

1. _____

2. _____

3. _____

Journaling. Happy Stuff. Photos. (Or extra Gratitude!)

Daily Journal - Day 230 / 136

Today is _____ / _____ / _____

My Gratitudes:

1. _____

2. _____

3. _____

My Gratitude Intentions - Setting my GPS / SAT NAV:

1. _____

2. _____

3. _____

Journaling. Happy Stuff. Photos. (Or extra Gratitude!)

Daily Journal - Day 231 / 135

Today is _____ / _____ / _____

My Gratitudes:

1. _____

2. _____

3. _____

My Gratitude Intentions - Setting my GPS / SAT NAV:

1. _____

2. _____

3. _____

Journaling. Happy Stuff. Photos. (Or extra Gratitude!)

Daily Journal - Day 232 / 134

Today is _____ / _____ / _____

My Gratitudes:

1. _____

2. _____

3. _____

My Gratitude Intentions - Setting my GPS / SAT NAV:

1. _____

2. _____

3. _____

Journaling. Happy Stuff. Photos. (Or extra Gratitude!)

Ignorance held me back. Now I can launch my freedom out enthusiastically
into the sea of opportunity in the sailboat of my life.

Daily Journal - Day 233 / 133

Today is _____ / _____ / _____

My Gratitudes:

1. _____

2. _____

3. _____

My Gratitude Intentions - Setting my GPS / SAT NAV:

1. _____

2. _____

3. _____

Journaling. Happy Stuff. Photos. (Or extra Gratitude!)

Daily Journal - Day 234 / 132

Today is _____ / _____ / _____

My Gratitudes:

1. _____

2. _____

3. _____

My Gratitude Intentions - Setting my GPS / SAT NAV:

1. _____

2. _____

3. _____

Journaling. Happy Stuff. Photos. (Or extra Gratitude!)

Daily Journal - Day 235 / 131

Today is _____ / _____ / _____

My Gratitudes:

1. _____

2. _____

3. _____

My Gratitude Intentions - Setting my GPS / SAT NAV:

1. _____

2. _____

3. _____

Journaling. Happy Stuff. Photos. (Or extra Gratitude!)

Daily Journal - Day 236 / 130

Today is _____ / _____ / _____

My Gratitudes:

1. _____

2. _____

3. _____

My Gratitude Intentions - Setting my GPS / SAT NAV:

1. _____

2. _____

3. _____

Journaling. Happy Stuff. Photos. (Or extra Gratitude!)

Daily Journal - Day 237 / 129

Today is _____ / _____ / _____

My Gratitudes:

1. _____

2. _____

3. _____

My Gratitude Intentions - Setting my GPS / SAT NAV:

1. _____

2. _____

3. _____

Journaling. Happy Stuff. Photos. (Or extra Gratitude!)

Daily Journal - Day 238 / 128

Today is _____ / _____ / _____

My Gratitudes:

1. _____

2. _____

3. _____

My Gratitude Intentions - Setting my GPS / SAT NAV:

1. _____

2. _____

3. _____

Journaling. Happy Stuff. Photos. (Or extra Gratitude!)

Give glory to the vibrant feel good all around.
Seek it out! Connect to it! Light up! Give light! Show the way!

Daily Journal - Day 239 / 127

Today is _____ / _____ / _____

My Gratitudes:

1. _____

2. _____

3. _____

My Gratitude Intentions - Setting my GPS / SAT NAV:

1. _____

2. _____

3. _____

Journaling. Happy Stuff. Photos. (Or extra Gratitude!)

Daily Journal - Day 240 / 126

Today is _____ /_____ /_____

My Gratitudes:

1. _____

2. _____

3. _____

My Gratitude Intentions - Setting my GPS / SAT NAV:

1. _____

2. _____

3. _____

Journaling. Happy Stuff. Photos. (Or extra Gratitude!)

Daily Journal - Day 241 / 125

Today is _____ / _____ / _____

My Gratitudes:

1. _____

2. _____

3. _____

My Gratitude Intentions - Setting my GPS / SAT NAV:

1. _____

2. _____

3. _____

Journaling. Happy Stuff. Photos. (Or extra Gratitude!)

Daily Journal - Day 242 / 124

Today is _____ / _____ / _____

My Gratitudes:

1. _____

2. _____

3. _____

My Gratitude Intentions - Setting my GPS / SAT NAV:

1. _____

2. _____

3. _____

Journaling. Happy Stuff. Photos. (Or extra Gratitude!)

Daily Journal - Day 243 / 123

Today is _____ / _____ / _____

My Gratitudes:

1. _____

2. _____

3. _____

My Gratitude Intentions - Setting my GPS / SAT NAV:

1. _____

2. _____

3. _____

Journaling. Happy Stuff. Photos. (Or extra Gratitude!)

Daily Journal - Day 244 / 122

Today is _____ / _____ / _____

My Gratitudes:

1. _____

2. _____

3. _____

My Gratitude Intentions - Setting my GPS / SAT NAV:

1. _____

2. _____

3. _____

Journaling. Happy Stuff. Photos. (Or extra Gratitude!)

DESIRE! Delicious desire drives the quality of my life forward,
bringing into view endless opportunity and abundance of adventure!

Daily Journal - Day 245 / 121

Today is _____ / _____ / _____

My Gratitudes:

1. _____

2. _____

3. _____

My Gratitude Intentions - Setting my GPS / SAT NAV:

1. _____

2. _____

3. _____

Journaling. Happy Stuff. Photos. (Or extra Gratitude!)

Daily Journal - Day 246 / 120

Today is _____ / _____ / _____

My Gratitudes:

1. _____

2. _____

3. _____

My Gratitude Intentions - Setting my GPS / SAT NAV:

1. _____

2. _____

3. _____

Journaling. Happy Stuff. Photos. (Or extra Gratitude!)

Daily Journal - Day 247 / 119

Today is _____ / _____ / _____

My Gratitudes:

1. _____

2. _____

3. _____

My Gratitude Intentions - Setting my GPS / SAT NAV:

1. _____

2. _____

3. _____

Journaling. Happy Stuff. Photos. (Or extra Gratitude!)

Daily Journal - Day 248 / 118

Today is _____ / _____ / _____

My Gratitudes:

1. _____

2. _____

3. _____

My Gratitude Intentions - Setting my GPS / SAT NAV:

1. _____

2. _____

3. _____

Journaling. Happy Stuff. Photos. (Or extra Gratitude!)

Daily Journal - Day 249 / 117

Today is _____ / _____ / _____

My Gratitudes:

1. _____

2. _____

3. _____

My Gratitude Intentions - Setting my GPS / SAT NAV:

1. _____

2. _____

3. _____

Journaling. Happy Stuff. Photos. (Or extra Gratitude!)

Daily Journal - Day 250 / 116

Today is _____ / _____ / _____

My Gratitudes:

1. _____

2. _____

3. _____

My Gratitude Intentions - Setting my GPS / SAT NAV:

1. _____

2. _____

3. _____

Journaling. Happy Stuff. Photos. (Or extra Gratitude!)

When I attach my dreams to my vision of the possible, I take up my place in the plan and claim my birthright from the Universal Deity.

Daily Journal - Day 251 / 115

Today is _____ / _____ / _____

My Gratitudes:

1. _____

2. _____

3. _____

My Gratitude Intentions - Setting my GPS / SAT NAV:

1. _____

2. _____

3. _____

Journaling. Happy Stuff. Photos. (Or extra Gratitude!)

Daily Journal - Day 252 / 114

Today is _____ / _____ / _____

My Gratitudes:

1. _____

2. _____

3. _____

My Gratitude Intentions - Setting my GPS / SAT NAV:

1. _____

2. _____

3. _____

Journaling. Happy Stuff. Photos. (Or extra Gratitude!)

Daily Journal - Day 253 / 113

Today is _____ / _____ / _____

My Gratitudes:

1. _____

2. _____

3. _____

My Gratitude Intentions - Setting my GPS / SAT NAV:

1. _____

2. _____

3. _____

Journaling. Happy Stuff. Photos. (Or extra Gratitude!)

Daily Journal - Day 254 / 112

Today is _____ / _____ / _____

My Gratitudes:

1. _____

2. _____

3. _____

My Gratitude Intentions - Setting my GPS / SAT NAV:

1. _____

2. _____

3. _____

Journaling. Happy Stuff. Photos. (Or extra Gratitude!)

Daily Journal - Day 255 / 111

Today is _____ / _____ / _____

My Gratitudes:

1. _____

2. _____

3. _____

My Gratitude Intentions - Setting my GPS / SAT NAV:

1. _____

2. _____

3. _____

Journaling. Happy Stuff. Photos. (Or extra Gratitude!)

Daily Journal - Day 256 / 110

Today is _____ / _____ / _____

My Gratitudes:

1. _____

2. _____

3. _____

My Gratitude Intentions - Setting my GPS / SAT NAV:

1. _____

2. _____

3. _____

Journaling. Happy Stuff. Photos. (Or extra Gratitude!)

Golden streams of the 14-karat caliber shower down on my
life, only when I allow them to.

Daily Journal - Day 257 / 109

Today is _____ / _____ / _____

My Gratitudes:

1. _____

2. _____

3. _____

My Gratitude Intentions - Setting my GPS / SAT NAV:

1. _____

2. _____

3. _____

Journaling. Happy Stuff. Photos. (Or extra Gratitude!)

Daily Journal - Day 258 / 108

Today is _____ / _____ / _____

My Gratitudes:

1. _____

2. _____

3. _____

My Gratitude Intentions - Setting my GPS / SAT NAV:

1. _____

2. _____

3. _____

Journaling. Happy Stuff. Photos. (Or extra Gratitude!)

Daily Journal - Day 259 / 107

Today is _____ / _____ / _____

My Gratitudes:

1. _____

2. _____

3. _____

My Gratitude Intentions - Setting my GPS / SAT NAV:

1. _____

2. _____

3. _____

Journaling. Happy Stuff. Photos. (Or extra Gratitude!)

Daily Journal - Day 260 / 106

Today is _____ / _____ / _____

My Gratitudes:

1. _____

2. _____

3. _____

My Gratitude Intentions - Setting my GPS / SAT NAV:

1. _____

2. _____

3. _____

Journaling. Happy Stuff. Photos. (Or extra Gratitude!)

Daily Journal - Day 261 / 105

Today is _____ / _____ / _____

My Gratitudes:

1. _____

2. _____

3. _____

My Gratitude Intentions - Setting my GPS / SAT NAV:

1. _____

2. _____

3. _____

Journaling. Happy Stuff. Photos. (Or extra Gratitude!)

Daily Journal - Day 262 / 104

Today is _____ /_____ /_____

My Gratitudes:

1. _____

2. _____

3. _____

My Gratitude Intentions - Setting my GPS / SAT NAV:

1. _____

2. _____

3. _____

Journaling. Happy Stuff. Photos. (Or extra Gratitude!)

The abundance of opportunity twitches with eager anticipation in the wings
of my life, watching for the simple nod of my permission to bounce on
to the stage filling it with sheer joy of being.

Daily Journal - Day 263 / 103

Today is _____ / _____ / _____

My Gratitudes:

1. _____

2. _____

3. _____

My Gratitude Intentions - Setting my GPS / SAT NAV:

1. _____

2. _____

3. _____

Journaling. Happy Stuff. Photos. (Or extra Gratitude!)

Daily Journal - Day 264 / 102

Today is _____ /_____ /_____

My Gratitudes:

1. _____

2. _____

3. _____

My Gratitude Intentions - Setting my GPS / SAT NAV:

1. _____

2. _____

3. _____

Journaling. Happy Stuff. Photos. (Or extra Gratitude!)

Daily Journal - Day 265 / 101

Today is _____ / _____ / _____

My Gratitudes:

1. _____

2. _____

3. _____

My Gratitude Intentions - Setting my GPS / SAT NAV:

1. _____

2. _____

3. _____

Journaling. Happy Stuff. Photos. (Or extra Gratitude!)

Daily Journal - Day 266 / 100

Today is _____ / _____ / _____

My Gratitudes:

1. _____

2. _____

3. _____

My Gratitude Intentions - Setting my GPS / SAT NAV:

1. _____

2. _____

3. _____

Journaling. Happy Stuff. Photos. (Or extra Gratitude!)

Daily Journal - Day 267 / 99

Today is _____ / _____ / _____

My Gratitudes:

1. _____

2. _____

3. _____

My Gratitude Intentions - Setting my GPS / SAT NAV:

1. _____

2. _____

3. _____

Journaling. Happy Stuff. Photos. (Or extra Gratitude!)

Daily Journal - Day 268 / 98

Today is _____ / _____ / _____

My Gratitudes:

1. _____

2. _____

3. _____

My Gratitude Intentions - Setting my GPS / SAT NAV:

1. _____

2. _____

3. _____

Journaling. Happy Stuff. Photos. (Or extra Gratitude!)

Determination is the driver which, when I engage in it, will reward my life with the greatest potency of love and brightest light of joy.

Daily Journal - Day 269 / 97

Today is _____ / _____ / _____

My Gratitudes:

1. _____

2. _____

3. _____

My Gratitude Intentions - Setting my GPS / SAT NAV:

1. _____

2. _____

3. _____

Journaling. Happy Stuff. Photos. (Or extra Gratitude!)

Daily Journal - Day 270 / 96

Today is _____ / _____ / _____

My Gratitudes:

1. _____

2. _____

3. _____

My Gratitude Intentions - Setting my GPS / SAT NAV:

1. _____

2. _____

3. _____

Journaling. Happy Stuff. Photos. (Or extra Gratitude!)

Daily Journal - Day 271 / 95

Today is _____ / _____ / _____

My Gratitudes:

1. _____

2. _____

3. _____

My Gratitude Intentions - Setting my GPS / SAT NAV:

1. _____

2. _____

3. _____

Journaling. Happy Stuff. Photos. (Or extra Gratitude!)

Daily Journal - Day 272 / 94

Today is _____ / _____ / _____

My Gratitudes:

1. _____

2. _____

3. _____

My Gratitude Intentions - Setting my GPS / SAT NAV:

1. _____

2. _____

3. _____

Journaling. Happy Stuff. Photos. (Or extra Gratitude!)

Daily Journal - Day 273 / 93

Today is _____ / _____ / _____

My Gratitudes:

1. _____

2. _____

3. _____

My Gratitude Intentions - Setting my GPS / SAT NAV:

1. _____

2. _____

3. _____

Journaling. Happy Stuff. Photos. (Or extra Gratitude!)

Daily Journal - Day 274 / 92

Today is _____ /_____ /_____

My Gratitudes:

1. _____

2. _____

3. _____

My Gratitude Intentions - Setting my GPS / SAT NAV:

1. _____

2. _____

3. _____

Journaling. Happy Stuff. Photos. (Or extra Gratitude!)

When I finally stop and recover my resources I uncover my unique and infinite treasure, claim my true inheritance and prepare to discover unbridled abundance.

Daily Journal - Day 275 / 91

Today is _____ / _____ / _____

My Gratitudes:

1. _____

2. _____

3. _____

My Gratitude Intentions - Setting my GPS / SAT NAV:

1. _____

2. _____

3. _____

Journaling. Happy Stuff. Photos. (Or extra Gratitude!)

Daily Journal - Day 276 / 90

Today is _____ / _____ / _____

My Gratitudes:

1. _____

2. _____

3. _____

My Gratitude Intentions - Setting my GPS / SAT NAV:

1. _____

2. _____

3. _____

Journaling. Happy Stuff. Photos. (Or extra Gratitude!)

Daily Journal - Day 277 / 89

Today is _____ / _____ / _____

My Gratitudes:

1. _____

2. _____

3. _____

My Gratitude Intentions - Setting my GPS / SAT NAV:

1. _____

2. _____

3. _____

Journaling. Happy Stuff. Photos. (Or extra Gratitude!)

Daily Journal - Day 278 / 88

Today is _____ / _____ / _____

My Gratitudes:

1. _____

2. _____

3. _____

My Gratitude Intentions - Setting my GPS / SAT NAV:

1. _____

2. _____

3. _____

Journaling. Happy Stuff. Photos. (Or extra Gratitude!)

Daily Journal - Day 279 / 87

Today is _____ / _____ / _____

My Gratitudes:

1. _____

2. _____

3. _____

My Gratitude Intentions - Setting my GPS / SAT NAV:

1. _____

2. _____

3. _____

Journaling. Happy Stuff. Photos. (Or extra Gratitude!)

Daily Journal - Day 280 / 86

Today is _____ /_____ /_____

My Gratitudes:

1. _____

2. _____

3. _____

My Gratitude Intentions - Setting my GPS / SAT NAV:

1. _____

2. _____

3. _____

Journaling. Happy Stuff. Photos. (Or extra Gratitude!)

Listen for the melody in the gentle rhythm of my beating heart and
rest in the comfort of my connection to the universe.

Daily Journal - Day 281 / 85

Today is _____ / _____ / _____

My Gratitudes:

1. _____

2. _____

3. _____

My Gratitude Intentions - Setting my GPS / SAT NAV:

1. _____

2. _____

3. _____

Journaling. Happy Stuff. Photos. (Or extra Gratitude!)

Daily Journal - Day 282 / 84

Today is _____ /_____ /_____

My Gratitudes:

1. _____

2. _____

3. _____

My Gratitude Intentions - Setting my GPS / SAT NAV:

1. _____

2. _____

3. _____

Journaling. Happy Stuff. Photos. (Or extra Gratitude!)

Daily Journal - Day 283 / 83

Today is _____ / _____ / _____

My Gratitudes:

1. _____

2. _____

3. _____

My Gratitude Intentions - Setting my GPS / SAT NAV:

1. _____

2. _____

3. _____

Journaling. Happy Stuff. Photos. (Or extra Gratitude!)

Daily Journal - Day 284 / 82

Today is _____ / _____ / _____

My Gratitudes:

1. _____

2. _____

3. _____

My Gratitude Intentions - Setting my GPS / SAT NAV:

1. _____

2. _____

3. _____

Journaling. Happy Stuff. Photos. (Or extra Gratitude!)

Daily Journal - Day 285 / 81

Today is _____ / _____ / _____

My Gratitudes:

1. _____

2. _____

3. _____

My Gratitude Intentions - Setting my GPS / SAT NAV:

1. _____

2. _____

3. _____

Journaling. Happy Stuff. Photos. (Or extra Gratitude!)

Daily Journal - Day 286 / 80

Today is _____ / _____ / _____

My Gratitudes:

1. _____

2. _____

3. _____

My Gratitude Intentions - Setting my GPS / SAT NAV:

1. _____

2. _____

3. _____

Journaling. Happy Stuff. Photos. (Or extra Gratitude!)

Flip the thought and suddenly the power of my pure joy is ignited.
Once launched, it soars through the universe with the ecstatic
delight of a magical firework.

Daily Journal - Day 287 / 79

Today is _____ / _____ / _____

My Gratitudes:

1. _____

2. _____

3. _____

My Gratitude Intentions - Setting my GPS / SAT NAV:

1. _____

2. _____

3. _____

Journaling. Happy Stuff. Photos. (Or extra Gratitude!)

Daily Journal - Day 288 / 78

Today is _____ /_____ /_____

My Gratitudes:

1. _____

2. _____

3. _____

My Gratitude Intentions - Setting my GPS / SAT NAV:

1. _____

2. _____

3. _____

Journaling. Happy Stuff. Photos. (Or extra Gratitude!)

Daily Journal - Day 289 / 77

Today is _____ / _____ / _____

My Gratitudes:

1. _____

2. _____

3. _____

My Gratitude Intentions - Setting my GPS / SAT NAV:

1. _____

2. _____

3. _____

Journaling. Happy Stuff. Photos. (Or extra Gratitude!)

Daily Journal - Day 290 / 76

Today is _____ / _____ / _____

My Gratitudes:

1. _____

2. _____

3. _____

My Gratitude Intentions - Setting my GPS / SAT NAV:

1. _____

2. _____

3. _____

Journaling. Happy Stuff. Photos. (Or extra Gratitude!)

Daily Journal - Day 291 / 75

Today is _____ / _____ / _____

My Gratitudes:

1. _____

2. _____

3. _____

My Gratitude Intentions - Setting my GPS / SAT NAV:

1. _____

2. _____

3. _____

Journaling. Happy Stuff. Photos. (Or extra Gratitude!)

Daily Journal - Day 292 / 74

Today is _____ / _____ / _____

My Gratitudes:

1. _____

2. _____

3. _____

My Gratitude Intentions - Setting my GPS / SAT NAV:

1. _____

2. _____

3. _____

Journaling. Happy Stuff. Photos. (Or extra Gratitude!)

Honour my power of alignment, and my soul shuffles into perfect harmony with my Source. I anchor the core of my being with the pivotal forces of my heart's truest, highest essence.

Daily Journal - Day 293 / 73

Today is _____ /_____ /_____

My Gratitudes:

1. _____

2. _____

3. _____

My Gratitude Intentions - Setting my GPS / SAT NAV:

1. _____

2. _____

3. _____

Journaling. Happy Stuff. Photos. (Or extra Gratitude!)

Daily Journal - Day 294 / 72

Today is _____ / _____ / _____

My Gratitudes:

1. _____

2. _____

3. _____

My Gratitude Intentions - Setting my GPS / SAT NAV:

1. _____

2. _____

3. _____

Journaling. Happy Stuff. Photos. (Or extra Gratitude!)

Daily Journal - Day 295 / 71

Today is _____ / _____ / _____

My Gratitudes:

1. _____

2. _____

3. _____

My Gratitude Intentions - Setting my GPS / SAT NAV:

1. _____

2. _____

3. _____

Journaling. Happy Stuff. Photos. (Or extra Gratitude!)

Daily Journal - Day 296 / 70

Today is _____ /_____ /_____

My Gratitudes:

1. _____

2. _____

3. _____

My Gratitude Intentions - Setting my GPS / SAT NAV:

1. _____

2. _____

3. _____

Journaling. Happy Stuff. Photos. (Or extra Gratitude!)

Daily Journal - Day 297 / 69

Today is _____ / _____ / _____

My Gratitudes:

1. _____

2. _____

3. _____

My Gratitude Intentions - Setting my GPS / SAT NAV:

1. _____

2. _____

3. _____

Journaling. Happy Stuff. Photos. (Or extra Gratitude!)

Daily Journal - Day 298 / 68

Today is _____ /_____ /_____

My Gratitudes:

1. _____

2. _____

3. _____

My Gratitude Intentions - Setting my GPS / SAT NAV:

1. _____

2. _____

3. _____

Journaling. Happy Stuff. Photos. (Or extra Gratitude!)

Changing the thought changes my mind, changes how I feel,
which added up, changes my life.

Daily Journal - Day 299 / 67

Today is _____ /_____ /_____

My Gratitudes:

1. _____

2. _____

3. _____

My Gratitude Intentions - Setting my GPS / SAT NAV:

1. _____

2. _____

3. _____

Journaling. Happy Stuff. Photos. (Or extra Gratitude!)

Daily Journal - Day 300 / 66

Today is _____ / _____ / _____

My Gratitudes:

1. _____

2. _____

3. _____

My Gratitude Intentions - Setting my GPS / SAT NAV:

1. _____

2. _____

3. _____

Journaling. Happy Stuff. Photos. (Or extra Gratitude!)

Daily Journal - Day 301 / 65

Today is _____ / _____ / _____

My Gratitudes:

1. _____

2. _____

3. _____

My Gratitude Intentions - Setting my GPS / SAT NAV:

1. _____

2. _____

3. _____

Journaling. Happy Stuff. Photos. (Or extra Gratitude!)

Daily Journal - Day 302 / 64

Today is _____ / _____ / _____

My Gratitudes:

1. _____

2. _____

3. _____

My Gratitude Intentions - Setting my GPS / SAT NAV:

1. _____

2. _____

3. _____

Journaling. Happy Stuff. Photos. (Or extra Gratitude!)

Daily Journal - Day 303 / 63

Today is _____ / _____ / _____

My Gratitudes:

1. _____

2. _____

3. _____

My Gratitude Intentions - Setting my GPS / SAT NAV:

1. _____

2. _____

3. _____

Journaling. Happy Stuff. Photos. (Or extra Gratitude!)

Daily Journal - Day 304 / 62

Today is _____ /_____ /_____

My Gratitudes:

1. _____

2. _____

3. _____

My Gratitude Intentions - Setting my GPS / SAT NAV:

1. _____

2. _____

3. _____

Journaling. Happy Stuff. Photos. (Or extra Gratitude!)

Knowing that I always have choices and that I am responsible for my life is the single most empowering adjustment I can ever make.

Daily Journal - Day 305 / 61

Today is _____ / _____ / _____

My Gratitudes:

1. _____

2. _____

3. _____

My Gratitude Intentions - Setting my GPS / SAT NAV:

1. _____

2. _____

3. _____

Journaling. Happy Stuff. Photos. (Or extra Gratitude!)

Daily Journal - Day 306 / 60

Today is _____ /_____ /_____

My Gratitudes:

1. _____

2. _____

3. _____

My Gratitude Intentions - Setting my GPS / SAT NAV:

1. _____

2. _____

3. _____

Journaling. Happy Stuff. Photos. (Or extra Gratitude!)

Daily Journal - Day 307 / 59

Today is _____ / _____ / _____

My Gratitudes:

1. _____

2. _____

3. _____

My Gratitude Intentions - Setting my GPS / SAT NAV:

1. _____

2. _____

3. _____

Journaling. Happy Stuff. Photos. (Or extra Gratitude!)

Daily Journal - Day 308 / 58

Today is _____ / _____ / _____

My Gratitudes:

1. _____

2. _____

3. _____

My Gratitude Intentions - Setting my GPS / SAT NAV:

1. _____

2. _____

3. _____

Journaling. Happy Stuff. Photos. (Or extra Gratitude!)

Daily Journal - Day 309 / 57

Today is _____ / _____ / _____

My Gratitudes:

1. _____

2. _____

3. _____

My Gratitude Intentions - Setting my GPS / SAT NAV:

1. _____

2. _____

3. _____

Journaling. Happy Stuff. Photos. (Or extra Gratitude!)

Daily Journal - Day 310 / 56

Today is _____ /_____ /_____

My Gratitudes:

1. _____

2. _____

3. _____

My Gratitude Intentions - Setting my GPS / SAT NAV:

1. _____

2. _____

3. _____

Journaling. Happy Stuff. Photos. (Or extra Gratitude!)

Being accountable for my daily life, changes my perspective and rewards me with the addictive, dynamic potency of choice.

Daily Journal - Day 311 / 55

Today is _____ / _____ / _____

My Gratitudes:

1. _____

2. _____

3. _____

My Gratitude Intentions - Setting my GPS / SAT NAV:

1. _____

2. _____

3. _____

Journaling. Happy Stuff. Photos. (Or extra Gratitude!)

Daily Journal - Day 312 / 54

Today is _____ / _____ / _____

My Gratitudes:

1. _____

2. _____

3. _____

My Gratitude Intentions - Setting my GPS / SAT NAV:

1. _____

2. _____

3. _____

Journaling. Happy Stuff. Photos. (Or extra Gratitude!)

Daily Journal - Day 313 / 53

Today is _____ / _____ / _____

My Gratitudes:

1. _____

2. _____

3. _____

My Gratitude Intentions - Setting my GPS / SAT NAV:

1. _____

2. _____

3. _____

Journaling. Happy Stuff. Photos. (Or extra Gratitude!)

Daily Journal - Day 314 / 52

Today is _____ / _____ / _____

My Gratitudes:

1. _____

2. _____

3. _____

My Gratitude Intentions - Setting my GPS / SAT NAV:

1. _____

2. _____

3. _____

Journaling. Happy Stuff. Photos. (Or extra Gratitude!)

Daily Journal - Day 315 / 51

Today is _____ / _____ / _____

My Gratitudes:

1. _____

2. _____

3. _____

My Gratitude Intentions - Setting my GPS / SAT NAV:

1. _____

2. _____

3. _____

Journaling. Happy Stuff. Photos. (Or extra Gratitude!)

Daily Journal - Day 316 / 50

Today is _____ / _____ / _____

My Gratitudes:

1. _____

2. _____

3. _____

My Gratitude Intentions - Setting my GPS / SAT NAV:

1. _____

2. _____

3. _____

Journaling. Happy Stuff. Photos. (Or extra Gratitude!)

Balance is the gem in the crown of my beautiful life, wherein
I control my peace with the wisdom of the benevolent sovereign.

Daily Journal - Day 317 / 49

Today is _____ / _____ / _____

My Gratitudes:

1. _____

2. _____

3. _____

My Gratitude Intentions - Setting my GPS / SAT NAV:

1. _____

2. _____

3. _____

Journaling. Happy Stuff. Photos. (Or extra Gratitude!)

Daily Journal - Day 318 / 48

Today is _____ / _____ / _____

My Gratitudes:

1. _____

2. _____

3. _____

My Gratitude Intentions - Setting my GPS / SAT NAV:

1. _____

2. _____

3. _____

Journaling. Happy Stuff. Photos. (Or extra Gratitude!)

Daily Journal - Day 319 / 47

Today is _____ / _____ / _____

My Gratitudes:

1. _____

2. _____

3. _____

My Gratitude Intentions - Setting my GPS / SAT NAV:

1. _____

2. _____

3. _____

Journaling. Happy Stuff. Photos. (Or extra Gratitude!)

Daily Journal - Day 320 / 46

Today is _____ / _____ / _____

My Gratitudes:

1. _____

2. _____

3. _____

My Gratitude Intentions - Setting my GPS / SAT NAV:

1. _____

2. _____

3. _____

Journaling. Happy Stuff. Photos. (Or extra Gratitude!)

Daily Journal - Day 321 / 45

Today is _____ / _____ / _____

My Gratitudes:

1. _____

2. _____

3. _____

My Gratitude Intentions - Setting my GPS / SAT NAV:

1. _____

2. _____

3. _____

Journaling. Happy Stuff. Photos. (Or extra Gratitude!)

Daily Journal - Day 322 / 44

Today is _____ / _____ / _____

My Gratitudes:

1. _____

2. _____

3. _____

My Gratitude Intentions - Setting my GPS / SAT NAV:

1. _____

2. _____

3. _____

Journaling. Happy Stuff. Photos. (Or extra Gratitude!)

Maximizing my positive attitude with the dynamic concentration of active responsibility releases the flow of energy into my life.

Daily Journal - Day 323 / 43

Today is _____ / _____ / _____

My Gratitudes:

1. _____

2. _____

3. _____

My Gratitude Intentions - Setting my GPS / SAT NAV:

1. _____

2. _____

3. _____

Journaling. Happy Stuff. Photos. (Or extra Gratitude!)

Daily Journal - Day 324 / 42

Today is _____ / _____ / _____

My Gratitudes:

1. _____

2. _____

3. _____

My Gratitude Intentions - Setting my GPS / SAT NAV:

1. _____

2. _____

3. _____

Journaling. Happy Stuff. Photos. (Or extra Gratitude!)

Daily Journal - Day 325 / 41

Today is _____ / _____ / _____

My Gratitudes:

1. _____

2. _____

3. _____

My Gratitude Intentions - Setting my GPS / SAT NAV:

1. _____

2. _____

3. _____

Journaling. Happy Stuff. Photos. (Or extra Gratitude!)

Daily Journal - Day 326 / 40

Today is _____ / _____ / _____

My Gratitudes:

1. _____

2. _____

3. _____

My Gratitude Intentions - Setting my GPS / SAT NAV:

1. _____

2. _____

3. _____

Journaling. Happy Stuff. Photos. (Or extra Gratitude!)

Daily Journal - Day 327 / 39

Today is _____ / _____ / _____

My Gratitudes:

1. _____

2. _____

3. _____

My Gratitude Intentions - Setting my GPS / SAT NAV:

1. _____

2. _____

3. _____

Journaling. Happy Stuff. Photos. (Or extra Gratitude!)

Daily Journal - Day 328 / 38

Today is _____ /_____ /_____

My Gratitudes:

1. _____

2. _____

3. _____

My Gratitude Intentions - Setting my GPS / SAT NAV:

1. _____

2. _____

3. _____

Journaling. Happy Stuff. Photos. (Or extra Gratitude!)

When I go first, I show the way to myself and then to the rest of the world.
Simply, I have made a difference.

Daily Journal - Day 329 / 37

Today is _____ / _____ / _____

My Gratitudes:

1. _____

2. _____

3. _____

My Gratitude Intentions - Setting my GPS / SAT NAV:

1. _____

2. _____

3. _____

Journaling. Happy Stuff. Photos. (Or extra Gratitude!)

Daily Journal - Day 330 / 36

Today is _____ / _____ / _____

My Gratitudes:

1. _____

2. _____

3. _____

My Gratitude Intentions - Setting my GPS / SAT NAV:

1. _____

2. _____

3. _____

Journaling. Happy Stuff. Photos. (Or extra Gratitude!)

Daily Journal - Day 331 / 35

Today is _____ / _____ / _____

My Gratitudes:

1. _____

2. _____

3. _____

My Gratitude Intentions - Setting my GPS / SAT NAV:

1. _____

2. _____

3. _____

Journaling. Happy Stuff. Photos. (Or extra Gratitude!)

Daily Journal - Day 332 / 34

Today is _____ / _____ / _____

My Gratitudes:

1. _____

2. _____

3. _____

My Gratitude Intentions - Setting my GPS / SAT NAV:

1. _____

2. _____

3. _____

Journaling. Happy Stuff. Photos. (Or extra Gratitude!)

Daily Journal - Day 333 / 33

Today is _____ / _____ / _____

My Gratitudes:

1. _____

2. _____

3. _____

My Gratitude Intentions - Setting my GPS / SAT NAV:

1. _____

2. _____

3. _____

Journaling. Happy Stuff. Photos. (Or extra Gratitude!)

Daily Journal - Day 334 / 32

Today is _____ / _____ / _____

My Gratitudes:

1. _____

2. _____

3. _____

My Gratitude Intentions - Setting my GPS / SAT NAV:

1. _____

2. _____

3. _____

Journaling. Happy Stuff. Photos. (Or extra Gratitude!)

To feel the invincible power of the subconscious truth in my body is to live with electrifying positivity and glorious joy!

Daily Journal - Day 335 / 31

Today is _____ / _____ / _____

My Gratitudes:

1. _____

2. _____

3. _____

My Gratitude Intentions - Setting my GPS / SAT NAV:

1. _____

2. _____

3. _____

Journaling. Happy Stuff. Photos. (Or extra Gratitude!)

Daily Journal - Day 336 / 30

Today is _____ / _____ / _____

My Gratitudes:

1. _____

2. _____

3. _____

My Gratitude Intentions - Setting my GPS / SAT NAV:

1. _____

2. _____

3. _____

Journaling. Happy Stuff. Photos. (Or extra Gratitude!)

Daily Journal - Day 337 / 29

Today is _____ / _____ / _____

My Gratitudes:

1. _____

2. _____

3. _____

My Gratitude Intentions - Setting my GPS / SAT NAV:

1. _____

2. _____

3. _____

Journaling. Happy Stuff. Photos. (Or extra Gratitude!)

Daily Journal - Day 338 / 28

Today is _____ / _____ / _____

My Gratitudes:

1. _____

2. _____

3. _____

My Gratitude Intentions - Setting my GPS / SAT NAV:

1. _____

2. _____

3. _____

Journaling. Happy Stuff. Photos. (Or extra Gratitude!)

Daily Journal - Day 339 / 27

Today is _____ / _____ / _____

My Gratitudes:

1. _____

2. _____

3. _____

My Gratitude Intentions - Setting my GPS / SAT NAV:

1. _____

2. _____

3. _____

Journaling. Happy Stuff. Photos. (Or extra Gratitude!)

Daily Journal - Day 340 / 26

Today is _____ / _____ / _____

My Gratitudes:

1. _____

2. _____

3. _____

My Gratitude Intentions - Setting my GPS / SAT NAV:

1. _____

2. _____

3. _____

Journaling. Happy Stuff. Photos. (Or extra Gratitude!)

*As I let go of my past I can forgive them but most of all I grant pardon
to myself and move forward with my life in a deeply splendid way.*

Daily Journal - Day 341 / 25

Today is _____ /_____ /_____

My Gratitudes:

1. _____

2. _____

3. _____

My Gratitude Intentions - Setting my GPS / SAT NAV:

1. _____

2. _____

3. _____

Journaling. Happy Stuff. Photos. (Or extra Gratitude!)

Daily Journal - Day 342 / 24

Today is _____ / _____ / _____

My Gratitudes:

1. _____

2. _____

3. _____

My Gratitude Intentions - Setting my GPS / SAT NAV:

1. _____

2. _____

3. _____

Journaling. Happy Stuff. Photos. (Or extra Gratitude!)

Daily Journal - Day 343 / 23

Today is _____ / _____ / _____

My Gratitudes:

1. _____

2. _____

3. _____

My Gratitude Intentions - Setting my GPS / SAT NAV:

1. _____

2. _____

3. _____

Journaling. Happy Stuff. Photos. (Or extra Gratitude!)

Daily Journal - Day 344 / 22

Today is _____ / _____ / _____

My Gratitudes:

1. _____

2. _____

3. _____

My Gratitude Intentions - Setting my GPS / SAT NAV:

1. _____

2. _____

3. _____

Journaling. Happy Stuff. Photos. (Or extra Gratitude!)

Daily Journal - Day 345 / 21

Today is _____ / _____ / _____

My Gratitudes:

1. _____

2. _____

3. _____

My Gratitude Intentions - Setting my GPS / SAT NAV:

1. _____

2. _____

3. _____

Journaling. Happy Stuff. Photos. (Or extra Gratitude!)

Daily Journal - Day 346 / 20

Today is _____ / _____ / _____

My Gratitudes:

1. _____

2. _____

3. _____

My Gratitude Intentions - Setting my GPS / SAT NAV:

1. _____

2. _____

3. _____

Journaling. Happy Stuff. Photos. (Or extra Gratitude!)

When I dare to go beyond fear of rejection and move into the excitement
of the unknown I know that I am rightly home.

Daily Journal - Day 347 / 19

Today is _____ / _____ / _____

My Gratitudes:

1. _____

2. _____

3. _____

My Gratitude Intentions - Setting my GPS / SAT NAV:

1. _____

2. _____

3. _____

Journaling. Happy Stuff. Photos. (Or extra Gratitude!)

Daily Journal - Day 348 / 18

Today is _____ / _____ / _____

My Gratitudes:

1. _____

2. _____

3. _____

My Gratitude Intentions - Setting my GPS / SAT NAV:

1. _____

2. _____

3. _____

Journaling. Happy Stuff. Photos. (Or extra Gratitude!)

Daily Journal - Day 349 / 17

Today is _____ / _____ / _____

My Gratitudes:

1. _____

2. _____

3. _____

My Gratitude Intentions - Setting my GPS / SAT NAV:

1. _____

2. _____

3. _____

Journaling. Happy Stuff. Photos. (Or extra Gratitude!)

Daily Journal - Day 350 / 16

Today is _____ / _____ / _____

My Gratitudes:

1. _____

2. _____

3. _____

My Gratitude Intentions - Setting my GPS / SAT NAV:

1. _____

2. _____

3. _____

Journaling. Happy Stuff. Photos. (Or extra Gratitude!)

Daily Journal - Day 351 / 15

Today is _____ / _____ / _____

My Gratitudes:

1. _____

2. _____

3. _____

My Gratitude Intentions - Setting my GPS / SAT NAV:

1. _____

2. _____

3. _____

Journaling. Happy Stuff. Photos. (Or extra Gratitude!)

Daily Journal - Day 352 / 14

Today is _____ / _____ / _____

My Gratitudes:

1. _____

2. _____

3. _____

My Gratitude Intentions - Setting my GPS / SAT NAV:

1. _____

2. _____

3. _____

Journaling. Happy Stuff. Photos. (Or extra Gratitude!)

As I come to know they could not teach me what they did not know,
could never give me what they did not have, the peace of authentic
freedom reposes easily on my soul.

Daily Journal - Day 353 / 13

Today is _____ / _____ / _____

My Gratitudes:

1. _____

2. _____

3. _____

My Gratitude Intentions - Setting my GPS / SAT NAV:

1. _____

2. _____

3. _____

Journaling. Happy Stuff. Photos. (Or extra Gratitude!)

Daily Journal - Day 354 / 122

Today is _____ / _____ / _____

My Gratitudes:

1. _____

2. _____

3. _____

My Gratitude Intentions - Setting my GPS / SAT NAV:

1. _____

2. _____

3. _____

Journaling. Happy Stuff. Photos. (Or extra Gratitude!)

Daily Journal - Day 355 / 11

Today is _____ / _____ / _____

My Gratitudes:

1. _____

2. _____

3. _____

My Gratitude Intentions - Setting my GPS / SAT NAV:

1. _____

2. _____

3. _____

Journaling. Happy Stuff. Photos. (Or extra Gratitude!)

Daily Journal - Day 356 / 10

Today is _____ / _____ / _____

My Gratitudes:

1. _____

2. _____

3. _____

My Gratitude Intentions - Setting my GPS / SAT NAV:

1. _____

2. _____

3. _____

Journaling. Happy Stuff. Photos. (Or extra Gratitude!)

Daily Journal - Day 357 / 9

Today is _____ / _____ / _____

My Gratitudes:

1. _____

2. _____

3. _____

My Gratitude Intentions - Setting my GPS / SAT NAV:

1. _____

2. _____

3. _____

Journaling. Happy Stuff. Photos. (Or extra Gratitude!)

Daily Journal - Day 358 / 8

Today is _____ / _____ / _____

My Gratitudes:

1. _____

2. _____

3. _____

My Gratitude Intentions - Setting my GPS / SAT NAV:

1. _____

2. _____

3. _____

Journaling. Happy Stuff. Photos. (Or extra Gratitude!)

Daily Journal - Day 359 / 7

Today is _____ / _____ / _____

My Gratitudes:

1. _____

2. _____

3. _____

My Gratitude Intentions - Setting my GPS / SAT NAV:

1. _____

2. _____

3. _____

Journaling. Happy Stuff. Photos. (Or extra Gratitude!)

Daily Journal - Day 360 / 6

Today is _____ / _____ / _____

My Gratitudes:

1. _____

2. _____

3. _____

My Gratitude Intentions - Setting my GPS / SAT NAV:

1. _____

2. _____

3. _____

Journaling. Happy Stuff. Photos. (Or extra Gratitude!)

Daily Journal - Day 361 / 5

Today is _____ / _____ / _____

My Gratitudes:

1. _____

2. _____

3. _____

My Gratitude Intentions - Setting my GPS / SAT NAV:

1. _____

2. _____

3. _____

Journaling. Happy Stuff. Photos. (Or extra Gratitude!)

Daily Journal - Day 362 / 4

Today is _____ / _____ / _____

My Gratitudes:

1. _____

2. _____

3. _____

My Gratitude Intentions - Setting my GPS / SAT NAV:

1. _____

2. _____

3. _____

Journaling. Happy Stuff. Photos. (Or extra Gratitude!)

Daily Journal - Day 363 / 3

Today is _____ / _____ / _____

My Gratitudes:

1. _____

2. _____

3. _____

My Gratitude Intentions - Setting my GPS / SAT NAV:

1. _____

2. _____

3. _____

Journaling. Happy Stuff. Photos. (Or extra Gratitude!)

Daily Journal - Day 364 / 2

Today is _____ /_____ /_____

My Gratitudes:

1. _____

2. _____

3. _____

My Gratitude Intentions - Setting my GPS / SAT NAV:

1. _____

2. _____

3. _____

Journaling. Happy Stuff. Photos. (Or extra Gratitude!)

Daily Journal - Day 365 / 1

Today is _____ / _____ / _____

My Gratitudes:

1. _____

2. _____

3. _____

My Gratitude Intentions - Setting my GPS / SAT NAV:

1. _____

2. _____

3. _____

Journaling. Happy Stuff. Photos. (Or extra Gratitude!)

CONGRATULATIONS!

Content Completion

Well Done! You made it! Now it's time to reflect on how far you've come and what you've achieved.

I would love to hear from you. Send me an email to: oppcompletion@deirdremaguire.com and I'll have a surprise for you!

Peace Always,

Deirdre

What's Next

To continue your journey, and to connect with like-minded people, join us through the following links:

Website:
www.deirdremaguire.com

Facebook:
www.facebook.com/wisdomofireland

Twitter:
@wisdomofireland

Subscribe to Our YouTube Channel (it's Free!)
www.youtube.com/wisdomofireland

Printed in Great Britain
by Amazon